Famous Women of the Reformed Church

HEIDELBERG IN 1620

Famous Women
of
The Reformed Church

James I. Good

Solid Ground Christian Books
Birmingham, Alabama USA

Solid Ground Christian Books
715 Oak Grove Road
Birmingham, AL 35209
205-443-0311
sgcb@charter.net
http://solid-ground-books.com

Famous Women of the Reformed Church

James Isaac Good (1850-1924)

Taken from 1901 edition by The Sunday School Board of the Reformed Church in the United States

Solid Ground Classic Reprints

First printing of new edition July 2007

Cover work by Borgo Design, Tuscaloosa, AL
Contact them at borgogirl@bellsouth.net

ISBN: 1-59925-123-X

Original Preface

The chapters of this book first appeared in the Reformed Church Magazine (1893-1895). They then received favorable comment. Since that Magazine ceased publication, there have been so many inquiries for them that it is evident they met a felt want in the Church, and the Sunday-school Board of the Reformed Church in the United States has undertaken their publication in this volume. The author has added several chapters to those that appeared in the Magazine. It is hoped that the lives of these Reformed saints will stimulate the ladies of our Church to greater interest in our splendid Church history, and to greater activity as in missions and the practical work of the Church, in which they already excel.

James I. Good
November 11, 1901

INDEX.

	Page
Part I. Women of the Reformation.	
Chapter I. Switzerland.	
Anna Reinhard, Zwingli's Wife	5
Calvin's Wife, Idelette D'Bures	21
Anna Bullinger	31
Chapter II. Germany.	
Catharine Zell	45
Margaret Blaarer	55
Chapter III. France.	
Queen Margaret of Navarre	59
Queen Jeanne D'Albret of Navarre	71
Charlotte D'Mornay	87
Phillipine De Luns	95
Charlotte D'Bourbon, Princess of Orange	103
Louisa De Coligny, Princess of Orange	113
Chapter IV. Italy.	
Duchess Renee of Este	125
Olympia Morata	135
Part II. Women of the Seventeenth Century.	
Chapter I. Germany.	
Electress Elizabeth of the Palatinate	149
Electress Louisa Juliana of the Palatinate	163
Landgravine Amalie Elizabeth of Hesse Cassel	171
Countess Ursula of Hadamer	177
Countess Gertrude of Bentheim	Opposite page 187

Duchess Cathrine Charlotte of Palatinate-Neuberg...
Opposite page 199
Princess Elizabeth of the Palatinate...Opposite page 205
Electress Louisa Henrietta of Brandenburg..........
Opposite page 221

Chapter II. Women of Other Lands.
Countess Susan Rakoczy of Hungary..Opposite page 237
The Women of the Tower of Constance.............
Opposite page 245

Chapter II. Women of Switzerland.
Anna Lavater........................Opposite page 253
Anna Schaltter and Meta Heusser Schweitzer........
Opposite page 273

Chapter IV. Women of America.
Mrs. Thomas C. Doremus...........Opposite page 285

ILLUSTRATIONS.

Heidelberg in 1620..........................Frontispiece
Zwingli Reading His Translation of the Bible to His wife
                                     Opposite page 11
Zwingli's Monument at Cappel............Opposite page 15
Zwingli's Daughter......................Opposite page 19
Queen Margaret Entertaining Reformed Refugees........
                                     Opposite page 68
Queen Jeanne D'Albret Addressing the Army...........
                                     Opposite page 80
Duchess Renee Defying Malicorne........Opposite page 131
Electress Louisa Juliana Interceding with Gustavus Adolphus.............................Opposite page 168
Landgravine Amalie Elizabeth............Opposite page 171
Electress Louisa Henrietta of Brandenburg............
                                     Opposite page 221
The Women of the Tower of Constance....Opposite page 245

PART I.

Women of the Reformation.

CHAPTER I.—SWITZERLAND.

I.

ANNA REINHARD, ZWINGLI'S WIFE.

THE wives of the Reformers are an interesting study. They receive greatness from their husbands, and impart gentleness and beauty in return. What would Luther have been without his Kathe? And Zwingli's wife is a helpmeet to him. The women of the Reformed Church have been an important element in her history. Just as Deborah and Esther, with the Marys of the New Testament, aided in making up Bible history, so the women of the Reformed Church have helped to make her history great.

We propose to give sketches of their lives in this volume. The first, and in some respects the most interesting of them, was the wife of the founder of our Church, Ulric Zwingli. Her name was Anna Reinhard. She had not been a nun like Catharine von Bora, Luther's wife. She was a pious widow when he married her. And there is an element of romance about their courtship which Luther's life does not have.

Not far from Zwingli's parsonage in Zurich was a house called the Hœfli. In it lived the widow of John Meyer, of Knonau. She was born about 1487, although the date of her birth is uncertain. Of her youth we know nothing, except that she was beautiful. Her hand was sought by a young companion, John Meyer von Knonau. But it happened that his father had chosen another bride for his son. The Knonau were among the oldest and most prominent noble families in Zurich, and John's father was proud of his family and position. He desired his son to occupy the same position in the aristocracy as he. So he sent him to the court of the bishop of Constance, his cousin, to be properly educated. And he chose as a bride for his son a lady of Thurgau, who belonged to a noble Austrian family. But his son was of a different mind. With true Swiss independence he preferred a Swiss girl to a foreign noblewoman. He had not forgotten the beautiful Anna Reinhard, the daughter of the landlord of the Rœssli, and they were secretly married in 1504 at a village chapel in the canton of Zurich. When the father heard of this, he became terribly angry. He forbade his son the house and disinherited him, leaving his fortune to his second wife, rather than to his son's family. Anna's husband was now cast on his own resources. He was elected to the city council in 1511 against his father's efforts, and then became ensign in the Swiss army, going with them to Italy in the wars against France. But after several campaigns he returned in broken health and died in 1517, leaving Anna a widow with three children, a son and two daughters.

Now it is her little boy Gerold around whom the romance of Zwingli's marriage seems to gather. He must have been a very beautiful and attractive boy, for his grandfather happened to be with some of the city councillors in a room that overlooked the fish-market one day, watching the people going to and fro. A maid came along with a little three-year-old boy and left him sitting at the stall while she paid for her fish. The old man noticed that the boy was attracting the attention of the passers-by by his beauty and pretty manners. He asked his companions, whose child the boy was, and was surprised to be told that it was the son of his son. He ordered the child to be brought to him and took him in his arms. The child, unabashed, played with his beard and looked him in the face so prettily, that the old man gave way to tears. He said to the boy, "Your father made me angry, but I will not let it injure you, but will take you as my child, instead of your father." And he ordered the boy to be taken to his own home, where the grandfather and grandmother cared for him with great tenderness. When he was nine years old his grandfather died, and his grandmother cared for him.

Now this beautiful boy, who so aptly healed over the breach in his father's family, was destined to do a similar act for Zwingli. It was this boy who unconsciously brought his mother and Zwingli together, until they were finally married. Zwingli came to Zurich after the death of his grandfather, when Anna was struggling to support and train her family, although she was cramped by her small means. She was from the beginning one of Zwingli's most attentive listeners, whenever he preached. As her home was in his parish, he came in contact with her as her pastor. He soon saw her needs and also her Christian graces. But it was Gerold who especially attracted his attention. Zwingli's quick eye soon saw the talents of this precocious boy. He gave him private lessons in Greek and Latin and when Gerold needed higher education, he sent him at the early age of eleven to Basle, then the literary centre of Switzerland. Thus Zwingli became a foster-father to the orphan. The boy was so bright that his teacher as Basle wrote back to Zwingli, "If you have any more such boys, send them to me. I will be a father to them, and they shall be my sons." When the boy went (1523) to the baths at Baden, instead of giving him the customary present, Zwingli gave him what was better. He wrote him a book, entitled "Directions for the Education of a Young Nobleman," and dedicated it to him.* Most earnestly he urged him to good morals and a Christian life. This beautiful and timely appeal saved the boy. He started out in a new life, and never after brought disgrace, but only honor on his family or friends. He became the brightest and most promising of the youth at Zurich—a member of the city council when only eighteen, and president of the city council at the early age of twenty-one. Although only a young man, he thus very rapidly rose to the highest

---

*A fine translation of this, the first Reformed work on education, has been made by Prof. A. Reichenbach, of Ursinus College, entitled "The Christian Education of Youth."

positions in the city. Now it was Zwingli's fatherly care over Gerold, his favorite, that prepared the way for his marriage with Gerold's mother. Gerold was, as her biographer says, the means of bringing his foster-father and his anxious mother together.

But there were grave difficulties in the way of the marriage, for it was not customary then for priests or ministers to marry. A priest had married in 1523 in Zurich, and it had caused a great commotion. Zwingli married Anna in 1522.* His marriage caused a great sensation, more in his birthplace in the Toggenburg than in Zurich. The Romanists and the Anabaptists charged him with marrying Anna for her beauty and her money. He replied that as for her money, she was not worth more than 400 guilders.

After marrying Zwingli, she ceased to wear jewelry. Zwingli addresses her as his dearest housewife, and such she was, a useful helpmeet in his work. She was a model minister's wife, the foster-mother of the poor, the visitor of the sick. She was

---

*Schaff says that a letter from Myconius to Zwingli would seem to show that Zwingli was married as early as 1522, but kept it secret for two years for fear of the opposition to it by the people. Myconius wrote to him in 1522 saying, "Farewell to your wife."

ZWINGLI READING TO HIS WIFE THE PROOF-SHEETS OF HIS NEW SWISS BIBLE

called "the apostolic Dorcas." Her care for her husband was greater even than for the parish. She brightened his cares and sympathized with him in his sorrows. When her husband, with the other ministers of Zurich, began translating the Bible (1525) and published it (1529) complete several years before Luther's complete Bible appeared (1534) it was his custom to read to her its proof-sheets every evening before retiring. She afterwards spoke of the eager interest she felt in the story of the gospel as it was thus translated into her own Swiss tongue by her husband. When it was published he presented her with a copy of it. The Bible thus became her favorite book. She tried to introduce it into the families of the congregation so that it might become the property of each household. When she found that her husband by early rising and excessive labors was becoming too deeply absorbed in his work, she would, as he says in a letter to Vadian, pull his sleeve and whisper in his ear, "Take a little more rest, my dear." In her intercourse with others she revealed the Christian's spirit. The more religious the conversation, the more she took part in it. No greater joy could come to her than to receive some new light on some holy truth. She loved to hear Zwingli in his homiletical works sometimes throwing new light on the character of Christ. She thus lived in a religious atmosphere. Toward her husband she always showed great reverence. Only one letter written by Zwingli to her has come down to us. It was written from Berne in 1528, just after a child had been born in his absence. It is a beautiful Christian epistle, thanking the Lord for the birth of a son, and praying that both parents might be able to educate him aright, urging her not to be anxious about his safety, and sending salutations to friends. He also wrote to her afterward from Strasburg when on his way to Marburg, when he praised the wife of Zell the Reformer, at Strasburg, of whom he said, "She combines the graces of both Mary and Martha." Anna welcomed his friends and entertained his guests, of whom there was always a large number. For Protestant refugees were many in those days, and Zwingli's house was always open to them. When Zwingli was engaged or away, she was the centre of the circle. The leading citizens and ministers like Leo Juda, Pellican and others, gave her great credit and praise. And the upper chancellor of Silesia, Arator, who visited Zwingli in 1526, was so pleased with the Christian arrangement of Zwingli's home, that he declared he would never forget it, and called Anna "an angel-wife." But her married life had not only pleasure and honor in it, but also care and anxiety. The danger in which her husband continually lived, gave her great care. He was repeatedly warned not to go out in the street alone at night, lest he be killed or carried off into a Catholic canton and suffer like Huss. He was also warned to be careful where he ate or drank, for fear he might be poisoned. Anna, when she noticed any danger at his side, would call for help. Frequently when her husband, especially in winter time, had to go through the streets after dark, she would call a citizen to accompany him. Or when he was kept in the corporation meeting late in the evening, she would try to arrange to have some friend accompany him home. She was always at his side or thoughtful of him when danger seemed near. Thus many attempts on his person, although near fulfillment, were frustrated. On August 28, 1525, their house was stoned by two citizens at night, the stones sending pieces of wood through the house. Anna and the family raised a great outcry. But Zwingli seized his sword and quieted them, calling out that if any one outside had any business they should come the next morning at daylight.

These anxieties were only prophecies of the still greater sorrow that was to come to her. She, with her husband, saw the black storm gathering over them, and which burst on the awful eleventh of October, 1531. For on the ninth the news came that the army of the Catholic cantons was approaching. Hastily a little army was gathered at Zurich against them. Zwingli was ordered to go along with them as chaplain. On the Charity Square just in front of the parsonage a part of the soldiers formed so as to depart. His wife came forth to bid him good-bye. Unable to repress her feelings she burst into tears, her children joining with her in weeping, clinging in the meanwhile to their father's garments so as to detain him, if possible, from danger. "The hour is come," he says to her, "that separates us. Let it be so. The Lord wills." He then gave her a parting embrace. Her fears almost robbed her of her speech, but she said, "We shall see each other again if the Lord will. His will be done. And what will you bring back when you come?" Zwingli's prompt reply was, "Blessing after dark night." These were his last words to her, and they remained as a

ZWINGLI'S MONUMENT AT CAPPEL

sacred comfort to her in all her after life. For she believed that blessing would come after the dark night of earth, as she saw him in the light of the new day in heaven. Zwingli then pressed his children to his heart and tore himself away. As he rode with the soldiers around the corner of the street, he looked back and she waved him a last good-bye. And now in her sorrow to whom should she go but to her Savior, to whom her husband had led her after he came to Zurich. She hurried into the house, and with the children threw herself down in the lonely chamber and prayed in the words of the Savior: "Father, not my will, but Thine be done." Comforted she arose and awaited the result of the battle. When the first news of the defeat, and of her husband's and her son's deaths came, her friends concealed from her the very sad particulars connected with it. They, however, hastened to comfort her. Prominent citizens and ministers visited her, sympathizing with her. Prominent ministers from other cities, as Capito and Bucer of Strasburg, and Keller of Augsburg, wrote beautiful letters of Christian sympathy. But the greatest comforter of all to her was young Henry Bullinger, her husband's successor. He now took her husband's place and cared for her as a son. He said to her: "You shall not want, dear mother. I will remain your friend, your teacher and adviser." Nor did he stop with words, but fulfilled them by deeds. Zwingli had left his family no means, for all he could spare he gave to the poor. So Bullinger took her under his own roof, at his own table, and united the two families into one. He also acted as a father to Zwingli's children, supervising their education and sending young Ulric to Basle at his own expense.

Of the later years of Anna we know almost nothing. It is said she rarely went out of the house after Zwingli's death, except when she went to church. She now lived for her children and for her Lord. In her later life she was very sick, and her disease continued for some years; but she bore her sufferings patiently.

Of her death on December 6, 1538, Bullinger says: "I desire no more happy end of life. She passed away softly, like a mild light, and went home to her Lord, worshipping, and commending us all to God." Her death was like her life—sweet, quiet, beautiful.

The most prominent scene in her life, and also the most impressive, is at the time of her husband's death on the battle-field at Cappel. Bullinger says that at the news of that awful defeat there arose in Zurich a loud and horrible cry of lamentation, and tears, bewailing and groaning. But her weeping was greater, her sorrow was deeper. The greater her husband, the greater her grief. She had had sorrows before, but this eclipsed them all. For his death was not her only sorrow then. With her husband there died on the battle-field her bright, beautiful son, Gerold. Nor was this all her sorrow. With her beloved husband and son there lay dead on that battle-field her brother and her brother-in-law, while a son-in-law was wounded unto death. The sadness of death compassed her about in all directions. And then came the news that her husband's body was quartered and burned, and its ashes desecrated. Was there ever sorrow like hers? Yes, there was One, of whom the prophet speaks: "Behold and see if there be any sorrow like unto my sorrow." To that Savior from sorrow she went in her sorrow, and He comforted her soul and raised up helpers to her. In one of her biographies there is a picture of her, weeping and in prayer, while a heavenly hand is reached down, wiping away her tears and beneath it is the text: "God will wipe away all tears from their eyes." In view of her great and many sorrows she might well be called the Mater Dolorosa, the weeping mother of the Reformation. Under her crosses she wept as Mary did at the cross. And just as John, the beloved disciple, took Mary to his home, so young Henry Bullinger gave Anna a home and became a beloved son to her.

The oldest daughter of Anna Zwingli, named Regula, inherited the beauty of her mother and possessed the piety of both her parents. She grew up in the family of Bullinger with young Rudolph Gualther, who afterwards became her husband and also the successor of her father and of Bullinger as the antistes or head of the Zurich church. During the Marian persecution in England, many of its refugees came to Switzerland and were entertained by her at her home, among them Grindal, later Archbishop of Canterbury, and others, who later became bishops of England. After her death her husband thus wrote of his loss, "What the pious Abraham lost in his beloved Sarah, and Jacob in his lovely Rachel, that have I also now to mourn. An example of purest love—of the most inviolable conjugal fidelity and domestic virtue, she knew how to drive away sadness and every tormenting care from my

REGULA ZWINGLI AND HER CHILD

soul." Her son, Rudolph, whose picture we show with hers, also later wrote a poem describing her fidelity, piety and other graces.

II.

CALVIN'S WIFE, IDELETTE D'BURES.

THE wife of Calvin is an almost unknown, but very interesting character, and worthy of a more prominent place among the women of the Reformed Church. Calvin did not think of marrying till he was thirty years of age, when he came to Strasburg, 1539. Then it was that he had more leisure to consider this important matter. His friends, too, urged him to marry. Well-meaning friends had anxiously concerned themselves about it long before he did, for he was over thirty years of age when he began to seriously consider it. An irate housekeeper drove him to seek for a wife. For she was so ill-tempered that one day she spoke to Calvin's brother, Antoine, with such impertinence that he left the house, saying he never would enter it again as long as she was there. Whereat she replied, "Then I am going, too," and she left Calvin, without any one to care for him. So as he wished to be freed from the petty worries of life, that he might give himself more fully to the work of the Lord, he began to search for a suitable person for a wife; or rather, he let his friends search for him, as he thought they knew better than he did. But he reserved for himself the final decision in the matter. He seems to have had several ladies recommended to him. "I was offered," he wrote to Farel, his closest friend, "a lady who was rich, young and of noble birth, and whose dower surpassed all that I could desire. Two things, however, urged me to refuse. She could not speak French, and it seemed to me she must be rather proud of her birth and education."

The main difficulty Calvin experienced was in the moral qualities of the person he sought. He looked beyond mere beauty of face or form, seeking beauty of soul. He says "he wished a wife who would be gentle, pure, modest, economical, patient, and to whom the care of her husband would be the chief matter;" probably owing to his poor health he felt especial need of the last named requisite. He evidently had a lofty ideal of the wife he wanted. Indeed, it has been said that his marriage was not so much of the heart as of the head, and made not through falling in love as much as being a business matter. He has, therefore, been charged with being a cold, though kind husband. This would in some sense seem natural to one like Calvin, who was so eminently intellectual. And yet D'Aubigne says, "This seems to me doubtful; when once married, he had a genuine affection for his wife. There was, we believe, a lofty intellect and a sublime genius, but also that love of kindred, those affections of the heart that complete the man."

These high ideals of Calvin only reveal how high must have been the character of Idelette De Bures (Van Buren) to be able to fulfil them. When Calvin had sought for a wife, until he was almost ready to give up, Bucer called his attention to Idelette, for Bucer had known her for her piety, her watchful tenderness and power of self-sacrifice as a wife, widow and mother. She had fled from Liege for the sake of her Protestant faith, and had married John Storder, who had been an Anabaptist, but both had been converted to the Reformed faith through Calvin's efforts. Calvin, therefore, had become acquainted with her before her husband's death. She, it seems, had been living so retired that he did not think of her at first. He, however, had noticed her deep-seated faith, devoted affection and Christian courage, that had led her to give up all for her faith. So Calvin proposed to her and was accepted.

The marriage took place August 1, 1540. It was

quite a large public wedding, some of the Swiss towns, as Neuchatel, being represented by deputies. Calvin's friends from France also took part in the wedding. Calvin was very happy after the wedding. He called Idelette "the excellent companion of his life, the ever faithful assistant of his ministry." He believed what the Bible says, "that whoso findeth a wife, findeth a good thing and obtaineth favor of the Lord." D'Aubigne calls attention to the fact that the reason why we know so much less about her than we do of Luther's wife, is because Calvin wrote less about her. And he did this purposely. For what Calvin prized most in his heart was her modesty. He, therefore, had such a sense of propriety that he did not obtrude her in his letters or his work any more than he would have thought of seeing her gadding about in the street. With him, too, everything was swayed by the thought of the work of Christ, and all his private and domestic affairs were eclipsed by this. For these reasons he wrote less about her than Luther, and therefore, unfortunately for us, we know less about her. But this very silence is in itself a beautiful tribute to her character.

Hardly had Calvin been married than he had to leave her. He was summoned to go to the conferences at Hagenau and Worms on account of political affairs. He left his wife at Strasburg in the care of his brother Antoine, and of a family named Richebourg, whose sons had been his pupils. Hardly had he gone, before the awful plague broke out in Strasburg. But duty to the Protestant cause, which was imperiled at these conferences, was stronger than duty to his family, and he could not come home. Meanwhile the plague raged violently. Young Louis De Richebourg and Claude Ferey, an intimate friend of Calvin's, soon died of it. Antoine, his brother, fled from Strasburg. Calvin in agony watched the mail for the news, fearing the worst for his wife. He wrote to a friend in Strasburg, "Day and night I see my wife before my eyes, who is in the midst of these dangers without help and advice, because her husband is away. I make great efforts to resist my grievous anxiety. I have recourse to prayer and holy meditation." His prayers were heard, Idelette's life was spared, and she was permitted to welcome him back to Strasburg. When Calvin was recalled to Geneva he left her at Strasburg. The council of Geneva sent three horses and a carriage to bring her and her household. They allotted a house with a garden attached to Calvin and his wife. There she revealed the same beautiful characteristics of a faithful wife. She was devoted to her husband. As he was naturally sickly and weak, she watched by his bedside in sickness, and cheered him in moments of weakness and depression. She thus greatly soothed him in the midst of the tremendous burdens of his labors. Doubtless we owe much of the abundance and clearness of his thoughts to her kind ministry in the home. Often she watched by his bedside at night, holding up his weary head, for he was a terrible sufferer of headache. In his sad hours, when adverse news came, she strengthened and comforted him. When the rebellious raged through the streets, crying out against the ministers of Geneva, she retired to her chamber, fell on her knees and prayed. Like a good pastor's wife she visited the sick. She was often seen comforting the sorrowing. Her house was an asylum for the numerous refugees who came crowding to Geneva. She cared for them with such beautiful hospitality that by some she was blamed for being more careful of strangers than of the natives of Geneva. She delighted in the company of his friends, especially of Farel, Beza, and others. She would accompany her husband on his walks, which he took only too rarely, to Cologny and Bellerive. Viret's wife was to her as a sister, and in May, 1545, when her husband went to Zurich, to stir up the German cantons to intercede for the Waldenses, she visited Viret's wife at Lausanne. But she had great sorrows, which brought much sickness. One by one her children were taken away from her by death in infancy. In July, 1542, she became very sick, and Calvin was greatly alarmed. He wrote to Viret, "I am in great anxiety." The next month her new-born babe died. Great was Calvin's grief. Writing to Viret, he says, "Salute all the brethren—salute also thy wife, to whom mine sends her thanks for the sweet and holy consolation which she received from her. She would write to acknowledge these with her own hand, but she had not strength to dictate a few words. In that He hath taken away our son, He hath stricken us sorely, but He is our Father. He knoweth what is meet for His children." Thus wrote Calvin, and yet he has been reproached as one whose heart was in his head, and as having no tender, deep feelings. Two years after this another child died, an infant daughter. And the next year another baby died. But like Rachel of old, Idelette mourned, and yet, unlike Rachel, she did not refuse to be comforted, for her consolation was that they were with Christ, which is far better. This sorrow was made all the greater because the Catholics claimed that their deaths were a judgment on them for being heretics. Calvin and his wife bore these reproaches with meekness, Calvin replying to them that though he had no natural children living, he had myriads of spiritual sons throughout the Christian world.

Her married life lasted only nine years. She never had been strong. In 1549 it was evident that she was becoming seriously ill. For three years she had suffered from fever, which with her sorrows had completely broken her down. Calvin now wrote to Viret, "I fear a fatal termination. The Lord will perhaps show us a more favorable countenance." His fears proved only too true. Although his wife had the best of physicians, Textor, who was a refugee and warm personal friend of Calvin's, yet all the physician's efforts failed to stay the disease. She gradually grew worse, and by April first her condition became so serious that all hope of cure was given up. Beza and others of Calvin's friends, as soon as they heard this, hastened to Calvin to comfort him. As she neared death, only one thing seemed to trouble her—her children of her former marriage to Storder. Calvin, seeing she was troubled, divining the reason, promised to treat them just as if they were his own children. At which she said, "I have already commended them to the Lord, but I know well that thou wilt not abandon those whom I have confided to the Lord." This last worldly care having been cast off her mind, she calmly waited for death. Although suffering very much, her face revealed the sweetness of the peace that reigned within. Her pastor Borgonius, who visited her on the evening of April 6, speaks of her simplicity of faith and elevation of hope as truly edifying. "O glorious resurrection," she exclaimed while he was speaking, and again, "O God of Abraham and of all our fathers, the faithful in all generations have trusted in Thee, and none have ever been confounded. I, too, trust in Thee from time to time." At six o'clock she said, as her friends had moved her to another bed and she was feeling very weak, "Pray, my friends; pray for me." Calvin drew closer to her; she still recognized him; he spoke to her of the grace of Christ and of that strength which was made perfect in weakness. He reminded her—though his voice faltered in doing so—of the blessed eternity of joy upon which she was about to enter. And then he prayed with her, commending her to Him in whom both believed. About 9 o'clock (April 5, 1549) she ceased to breathe, but so peacefully did she pass away that for some moments the watchers by her bedside were uncertain whether she slept or was dead.

Calvin, writing of her to Farel and Viret, says of her: "I have lost her who would never have quitted me either in exile, or misery, or death. She was a precious help to me, and never occupied with self. The best of partners has been taken from me." And seven years later, when writing to Valeville, the French pastor at Frankford, who had lost his wife, he says, "I know from my own experience how painful and burning are the wounds which the death of an excellent wife causes. How hard it has been to become master of my sorrows." Calvin, although duties pressed on him more than ever, never forgot Idelette—never for a moment thought of filling her place by marrying again. And when he pronounced her name, his tone and meaning revealed how dear she was to him. If her husband, who knew her best, could thus revere and honor her, it becomes us to honor her memory as one of the truest and most devoted of the wives of the reformers—a fit companion to Catharine Von Bora, Luther's wife, and Anna Reinhard, Zwingli's wife.

ANNA BULLINGER

III.

ANNA BULLINGER.

TWO women of the Reformed Church of the Reformation have been almost forgotten, and yet stand out as pre-eminently worthy of notice, for they were the Marthas of their day. Just as Martha was busy preparing a proper reception of Christ in her home, so these women, as they could not receive Christ personally into their homes like Martha, busied themselves greatly in receiving Christ's followers, and in receiving them, received Him. They were the wife of Zell, the first reformer of Strasburg, who received Bucer, Calvin, Farel and many more into her home, and Anna Bullinger. Their homes became in reality hotels, where the Protestant refugees found safety and a most kindly reception.

Anna Bullinger's maiden name was Adlischweiler. The date of her birth we do not know, but it was probably 1504. Her father died in battle when she was only eight years old. Her mother, thinking in her Romish blindness to do God a service, afterwards took her daughter and gave her to the Church by placing her in the cloister at Oedenbach, at Zurich, where she became a nun. And as the mother herself was sick with dropsy and desired to be near her daughter, she boarded there, too. But while they were thus quietly living in the cloister, strange things were happening outside of it in Zurich. The Reformation had come. Zwingli's preaching had won the town, and the Gospel was preached in the churches, until there was but one place in the town where it was not heard, and that was the nunnery at Oedenbach. Finally the city council of Zurich, unwilling that of all the inhabitants of the town the nuns there should be the only ones shut out from hearing a Gospel sermon, ordered Zwingli in 1522 to go and preach in the nunnery. This call he obeyed with great joy, and he preached a remarkable and impressive sermon on "The Clearness and Certainty of the Word of God." This sermon had a double effect. Some of the nuns were won by it to the Gospel, but others became very bitter against it. As a very bitter strife now broke out in the nunnery between the adherents and opponents of Zwingli, the city council at last felt itself compelled to forbid the Dominicans, who before had been the spiritual guides of the cloister, to enter it, and ordered Zwingli and Leo Juda to take the spiritual care of the inmates. Against this the monks and some of the sisters protested, but in vain. The council then gave orders, allowing any of the nuns, who so desired, to leave and to take their property and clothing with them. Many of them took advantage of this, and some who left married. Those who desired to remain, were permitted to do so, but were not allowed to wear nun's garb. Soon Anna was the only nun remaining in the nunnery, except one aged sister. And she would not have remained (for she had been won by Zwingli's preaching), but for the sake of her sick mother.

Now it happened that Leo Juda, who was chaplain of the nunnery, took with him one day young Henry Bullinger, who was on a visit to him. Bullinger's heart was touched by the tender influence of love, and he wrote her a marriage proposal. His letter to her is still extant as the first love letter of the Reformers. This letter is a long one,* covering fourteen and a half printed pages, and for candor and Christian love it might well be a model to all who desire to make marriage proposals (ex-

---

*See "Heinrich Bullinger und seine Gattin," by Christoffel, page 21.

cept that it is too long). In it he describes his physical condition and his means, and eloquently sums it up by saying, "But why are many words necessary! The sum of it all is, that the greatest, surest treasure that you will find in me, is fear of God, piety, fidelity and love, which with joy I will show you, and labor, earnestness and industry, which will not be wanting in temporal things. Concerning high nobility and many thousand gulden, I can say nothing to you. But I know that what is necessary to us, will not be wanting. For Paul says, 'We brought nothing into the world, and we will take nothing out. Therefore, if we have clothing and food it is enough.'"

Ten days after she received his proposal, Bullinger received her reply, which was in the affirmative. But as her mother was opposed to the marriage, and moreover was quite sick, Anna desired the marriage to be postponed, so that she could stay at the nunnery with her mother. Meanwhile Bullinger utilized the time by preparing her by careful teaching for her future position as his wife. He, therefore wrote a small book entitled, "Concerning Female Training, and How a Daughter Should Guide Her Conduct and Life." Her mother having

Anna Bullinger.

died, they were married in 1529. During the previous year Bullinger had been licensed by the Zurich Synod as a minister, and had accepted the pastorate at Bremgarten, where his father had been pastor. Two daughters were born to them there, and great was their joy. But it was soon turned into sorrow. For the defeat of Zurich at Cappel, on October 11, 1531, (in the battle where Zwingli fell) made it dangerous for them, especially for Bullinger, as the Romish armies had little mercy for Protestant ministers. So on the night of November 20 Bullinger fled from Bremgarten, together with his aged father and brother. They had hardly left the town, when the Catholic soldiers entered it and plundered Bullinger's house, and quartered thirty soldiers on Anna, who with the two little children had been left behind. She saw she could not provide for them, so she determined to flee, too. Now she had as her servant a woman, who because of her faithfulness has become a historical character. Her name was Brigette. She had served the family for many years, not for money, but for love, for her yearly wages were four gulden (about two dollars) and a pair of shoes, and yet for this she served the family for thirty-five years. Anna, leaving the care of the house to this faithful servant, fled with her two children, one a year and a half old, the other only six months old. When she came to the gate of the town, she found it closed and the guard was unwilling to open it. But nerved by a mother's superhuman strength, she wrested the key from him by force, and opened it and fled. Great was the joy of her husband, who was at Zurich, when she arrived safely with her little children, and glad were they to find a refuge at Zurich.

But they were still not perfectly safe, for after the defeat of Cappel and the death of Zwingli, there had come a reaction in Zurich, which had become so strong that Leo Juda, Zwingli's closest friend, was afraid to go out, and his wife trembled for his life. The church at Zurich was looking for a successor to Zwingli. Bullinger's friends, Leo Juda and Myconius prevailed on Bullinger to preach in the cathedral. And so able and eloquent was his sermon that the people said he was a Zwingli risen from the dead. The city of Zurich, finding he had calls to Basle, Bern and Appenzell, hastened to elect him, although he was only twenty-seven years old. Great was the honor shown him, but also great was the responsibility. His new position brought much honor to his wife but also many new cares. Not merely did her family grow almost yearly by the birth of a child until they numbered eleven, but as the wife of the head of the church, she had to receive and entertain many strangers in her house. Thus Bullinger's father and mother lived with them till they died. Bullinger also with great kindness took into his home the wife and children of his predecessor, Zwingli, and cared for them as he cared for his own family. He also received into his house young Rudolph Gualther and educated him. It was a kindness worthily bestowed, for Gualther afterwards became his successor as antistes. For Bullinger was fond of young men, and when he found one of bright mind and spiritual inclinations, he at his own cost reared and educated him. Thus in addition to Gualther he took Henry Lavater and Josiah Simler and others, and in 1531 two Polish boys with their tutor into his family. Thus Anna Bullinger's family became very large and her cares many. And the wonder is that on the small salary of 700 pounds she was able to do it.* Hence great

---

*It is true Bullinger had the interest of 700, which he inherited, and of his wife's estate of 2600—3300 in all. This at 6 per cent. interest would bring in 198, say 200, more. This would make his income only 900 pounds in all.

economy was necessary to feed and clothe so many in the family. Very characteristic was the letter Bullinger wrote to his oldest son at Strasburg, December 20, 1553, "Your mother makes big eyes when you already speak of needing another pair of shoes for the winter. It is hardly fifteen weeks since you left us, when you took three pairs with you, the red, the gray and black. At this rate you will need six pairs a year. I have more than enough with two." But Bullinger afterwards gives his son the advice, "Do not let your shoes go to pieces, but get them mended in time." And three months after he praises his son for his economy. On his small salary Bullinger could not have provided for all in his house had Anna not guided the household with her economy. Anna could not have borne all the cares had not Bullinger's mother aided her. And Brigette, too, greatly helped her, as Brigette had become more of a household companion than a servant, for Bullinger in writing to his son Henry in 1556, at Strasburg, says, "Your five sisters greet you, and especially Brigette, who sends to you a present of three groschen." Brigette might well be called the model servant of the Reformation. Little did she think that she would be spoken of 350 years after her tender ministry in Bullinger's home; but her faithfulness is worthy of it, and her life shows how one in a lowly position, only a servant girl, can gain a great reward by simple faithfulness, serving not for money but for love.

Thus Bullinger assisted by his wife was able to do much with little money. Nor were these things all the cares that came to Anna. Her house was not only a home to the homeless, but became virtually a sort of hotel, for to it came the refugees of every land. Zurich was an asylum to the persecuted Reformed of other lands. This was due to the great friendliness of Bullinger to the refugees. First in 1542 came the Italian Reformed, driven out by the persecutions of the inquisition, Peter Martyr, Bernard Ochino, Celio Curione, all scholarly, eloquent men. Curione writes a letter of thanks, in which he calls Bullinger a bishop according to the description of a bishop given by the apostle Paul, and says, "Your friendliness and your Christian care for us during our stay with you obliges me to give you my inmost thanks. Greet for us very heartily your wife, who showed herself so full of kindly service and love." Then came the refugees from Locarno, on the southern borders of Switzerland. Beccaria had there founded a Reformed church, and it had grown to two hundred members. Their prosperity incited their Catholic neighbors against them, and it was decided November 24, 1555, that all who would not return to the Romish faith must leave. So March 3, 1556, they fled over the snowy Alps, and one hundred and sixteen in number arrived at Zurich May 12. There they were gladly received by the people, and especially by Bullinger. He and his wife set the example and led the way. Great was her care and anxiety for those refugees, who had left all for the Gospel's sake. And when the fires of persecution broke out in England in 1550 under bloody Mary, Bullinger and the Zurich church gladly received them. Even before that, as early as 1536, Cranmer, the archbishop of Canterbury, had sent three young men to be educated at Zurich, one of whom Bullinger took into his own house, and the next year he took another. When they left, they kept up correspondence with him, and one of them, Partridge, again and again expressed his thankfulness to Bullinger and to his wife, who had become a mother to him. In 1546 Hooper, later bishop and martyr of the Church of England, came to Zurich, and was received by Bullinger in his own home, where he had a daughter baptized by Bullinger. After his return to England, he wrote to Bullinger, expressing his great thankfulness to him and his wife for their hospitality. When the Marian persecution broke out in England, Bullinger's table was often filled with refugees, and his wife often had great care and anxiety to know what to do with them, or how to provide for them. Zurich founded a school for them to educate twelve English students as ministers, of whom five afterwards became bishops. All of them afterwards expressed the greatest thankfulness to Bullinger and his wife for the kindness they had received at their house. They also sent presents to Zurich, as a return for kindnesses shown. There are still at Zurich three large polished silver goblets, which three of these returned bishops, Jewel, Horn and Parkhurst, presented to the church of Zurich. And there is also a goblet of fine workmanship, which Queen Elizabeth presented to Bullinger as a token of her thanks. Nor were these all the refugees entertained by Bullinger and his family. When the wars in Germany went against the Protestants, some of them found refuge at Zurich, as Musculus and Cellarius. Musculus, in a letter from Bern, afterwards thanks Bullinger for his hospitality, and also Bullinger's wife for the comfort of her letter to his wife.

Thus Bullinger's wife was a ministering angel to the refugees. Many were her cares and responsibilities, to which all these bear witness. In addition to these refugees there came many prominent foreign visitors, as Calvin and Farel from Geneva, also Bucer and Capito from Strasburg, among theologians, Portalis, the ambassador of the king of Navarre, the noble families of Wurtemburg and Schaumburg, who were refugees. All these were for a time entertained by Bullinger's family, or in social relations with it. And not only to foreigners was Bullinger's home a refuge for foreigners, but also to the poor at home. Thus Fabricius, the reformer of Chur, tells of a distant relative, who found herself poor and helpless at Zurich, and was taken by Bullinger to his own home and kept there for a time as a member of it. A continual stream of beautiful gifts flowed through the hand of Anna Bullinger to the huts of the poor and stilled many a grief. She provided the needy sick with food, drink, clothing, money, in fact everything necessary. She joined with the leading ladies of Zurich, the wives of ministers, as of Leo Juda, Pellican, Peter Martyr and others, in these labors of love. Is it any wonder, in view of all these things, that she was known at Zurich by the name, so descriptive of her character, of "mother." And in foreign lands, by English, Italians, Dutch and Germans, she was known and addressed by the title of "Zurich-mother." A good Samaritan was she till her end in 1564. Then her husband sickened of the plague, so that all thought he must die. During his sickness Anna, forgetful of self, nursed him so that he got well. But it was at the cost of her own life. For as he recovered, she sickened and died. Great was the sorrow in Zurich for her. And her memory remains for the Reformed as a beautiful inspiration for deeds of love and charity. "Blessed are the dead that die in the Lord from henceforth. Yea, saith the Spirit, that they may rest from their labors, and their works do follow them."

Chapter II.—GERMANY.

I.

CATHARINE ZELL.

AMONG the Reformed women of the Reformation none deserves greater credit than the subject of this sketch. She had her faults, it is true,—who has not,—but her faults were rather the excess of her virtues than anything else, for she was intense in her character. And she excelled all in being a mother to all refugees, and with her warm heart welcoming them to her house, which became a veritable "hotel" to them all her life.

Catharine Schutz (for such was her maiden name) was born in 1497 in Strasburg. She came from a prominent artisan family, and fortunately received from her parents an excellent education, which she was careful to use afterwards to aid her beloved faith. During her girlhood and school-days many changes were taking place at Strasburg. Gradually the doctrines of the Reformation were leavening the people. About 1518 Matthew Zell was called to be the preacher at the great cathedral there, and he soon began preaching the Gospel.

This caused a great excitement. The Romish archbishop, under whose care the cathedral was, refused to allow him to enter the pulpit any more. So as the pulpit was locked against him, his friends made for him a wooden pulpit, which they would carry into the church whenever he was to preach, and from it he preached to crowds which filled that vast church. As a result the city became largely Protestant under his preaching. Among his hearers was his future wife, Catharine Schutz, who readily accepted his doctrines with all the earnestness of her warm-hearted nature. She was married to Zell December 3, 1525. Martin Bucer, who was a later reformer at Strasburg than Zell (who was the first reformer of that city), married them. And at the close of the marriage ceremony they celebrated the Lord's Supper in the great cathedral after the Reformed manner. That immense building was filled mainly with men, who thus showed by their presence their approval of the marriage of a priest like Zell.

She proved to be a pious, busy, discreet wife, in the fullest sympathy with her husband. For this unity of feeling between them she often thanked God, and spoke of her husband and of herself frequently as "being of one mind and one soul." She says: "What bound us together was not silver and gold. Both of us possessed a higher thing, 'Christ was the mark before our eyes.'" As she was well educated, her progress in the Bible gave her a deep knowledge of religion. Endowed with rare courage and great natural eloquence, she understood how to defend her views by word, and even by pen if necessary. Her great aim was to spread abroad the Gospel. Sometimes it seemed as if she outdid her husband in this, so that he seemed to be placed in the background, and Bucer could shruggingly say that he was ruled by his wife. Yet Bucer himself bears witness that she was "as God-fearing and courageous as a hero." She herself says she wanted to be only the helpmeet of her husband, and a "little piece of the rib of the sainted Matthew Zell."

Her correspondence became quite large, and in it she excelled. Soon after her marriage she came into correspondence with Luther. She exchanged letters with Zwingli, and later with Bullinger, as well as Luther. She also filled her life full of good deeds, as caring for the sick and needy. And in this respect she excelled in caring for the refugees who fled to Strasburg because of persecution for their faith. She says: "I have already in the beginning of my marriage received many excellent and learned people in their flight, and comforted them as God has said: 'Support and strengthen the weak knees.'" When fifteen excellent men had to flee from Baden for conscience's sake, among them an old and learned man named Doctor Mantel, Zell took him into his house and gave him a home. After this kindly reception Mantel again fell into the hands of the Catholics, and lay for four years in prison, during which time his memories of Catharine Zell's kindness were a benediction to him. In 1524, 150 citizens in one night were driven out of the little village of Kenzingen in Breisgau, and came to Strasburg. Zell received eighty of them into his house, and Mrs. Zell kindly cared for them, feeding fifty or sixty for four weeks. She was continually busy in caring for such refugees, either herself, or by getting others to do it. Zell delighted in these labors of love of his wife. Many, very many were the refugees who received a warm welcome in their house. Among them Heilandt, of Calw, in Wurtemberg, who stayed there until he found a position at Strasburg. When in 1543 a number of poor scholars happened to gather together there, she was unwearied in getting supper for them. She took up collections for them and aided in housing them in the Williams cloister. Thus she entertained many of the greatest reformers who came as refugees. When Bucer, the greatest reformer of Strasburg, came fleeing from Weissenburg, he found a home and a refuge in Mrs. Zell's house. And again, when Calvin came fleeing from France, having had all his money stolen on the way, it was Mrs. Zell who gave him a warm welcome at her fireside. A peculiarly brilliant period of her life was the year 1529, when the conference between Luther and Zwingli at Marburg brought so many distinguished reformers to Strasburg. Like busy Martha of old, who entertained her Saviour with the best at Bethany, she exerted herself to entertain these noble followers of Christ. She said: "I have been for fourteen days maid and cook while the dear men Ecolampadius and Zwingli were here."

Her husband was inclined rather to quietness and peace, although he was not wanting in courage for the truth, as his boldness in being the first preacher of Protestantism in Strasburg shows. Still, while he was inclined to quietness in the controversies that raged around him among the Protestants, she was inclined to be controversial, and wielded her pen for the truth and for peace wherever she felt it was needed. She even wrote to Luther, asking him to treat the Swiss with a little more mildness in the controversy about the Lord's Supper. Luther replied to her quite politely and more mildly. After the Wittenberg Concord of 1536 had brought peace between Luther and the Swiss, Zell took a journey to Wittenberg, accompanied by his wife, of which trip she speaks in glowing terms. But while she was staunch for the truth, she was very liberal in her sympathies even toward the Schwenkfelders and Anabaptists. When Schwenkfeld, a Silesian nobleman, came as a refugee to Strasburg in 1528, he was received with kindness into her house. And when the younger ministers of Strasburg attacked him for his theological errors, she defended him in a public letter. They in reply reproached "Mrs. Doctor Catharine," as they called her, "with mental vagaries and obstinacy," and advised her, "rather to spin at the distaff and wait on the sick" than to engage in theological conflicts, which belonged rather to the clergy. Even after Schwenkfeld had been compelled to leave Strasburg, she remained in correspondence with him.

She was the author of a number of works. As

early as 1524 she defended Zell's conversion to Protestantism, and later his marriage to her. In that year, too, she published a work of comfort, "to her persecuted sisters of the congregation at Kenzingen," whose husbands had been driven away by the Austrians and had fled to Strasburg. In 1534 she wrote an introduction to a hymnbook. Her great labors aged her. However, she was still vigorous when the Lord called away her husband by death, January 9, 1548. On the last night of his life he called her to him and told her to give his last message to his assistant pastors, and ask them "to leave the Anabaptists and Schwenkfelders in peace, and to preach Christ rather than persecute them." It happened that the day of Zell's funeral was the day when the citizens renewed their oath to the city and elected their magistrates, and so three thousand men followed her husband to his grave. After Bucer had preached the funeral sermon and most of the people had gone home, she made an address to the intimate friends, in which she spoke of the pious labors of her husband and gave them his last words of love, urging them to peace, and to leave the Anabaptists and Schwenkfelders alone. The magistrates, out of respect to her husband, allowed her to remain living in the large parsonage of the cathedral, which she, as "mother of the Reformers" (as she was called), had consecrated by making it so often a spiritual asylum for refugees.

Then came sad days for her, when the Emperor tried to introduce the Interim (1547) with its Romish rites. She wrote a book, in which she bewailed this condition of affairs, and implored Strasburg to remain true to Christ and give up the Pope. With the death of Zell and the departure of Bucer for England, matters changed very much in Strasburg. Lutheranism was introduced. She had received into her home her husband's successor, Rabus, who became the most popular preacher of the city. He, although he had been trained in Zell's family, now began to attack the low Reformed views and customs, and to urge the introduction of high Lutheran methods. Mrs. Zell was not the woman to keep silent when her husband's acts and views were thus attacked, and she wrote against him. She therefore becomes *the great woman defender of the Reformed views in the Reformation.* Rabus answered her in 1557 from Ulm, where he was stationed. She replied in a letter to the whole citizenship of Strasburg. Her language was quite severe

Catharine Zell. 53

and her defence eloquent. She continued to be the refuge of the persecuted of all denominations. Thus in 1549, when Bucer and Fagius left Strasburg for London, as they bade her good-bye, they left in her hand two gold pieces, with the request that they be used for the refugees, if found necessary. This was a beautiful tribute from these great reformers to her kindness to the refugees. In her reply to them, she says she felt like doing to them what Joseph did to his brethren—return the money. She then, however, stated that a case had come to her notice of a persecuted minister with five children, and also another, of a minister's wife, before whose eyes the husband had been beheaded, both of them very needy. To these she had given one of the gold pieces, and the other she returned to them, thinking that they might need it themselves, as they would probably need much when they came to England. Thus she continued her labors of love till she died. The date of her death is not exactly known. She was living March 3, 1562, for then she sent an apology to Lewis Lavater, of Zurich, for not answering his letter, because she said "she was often half dead with her long sickness, and could not hold the pen." How soon after that she died is not known.

Such was the life and testimony of one of the foremost women of the Reformed Church in Reformation days. She is worthy of more notice than the silence of the past has given to her. Indeed, she may be said to deserve the title of the "Woman Reformer of the Reformed Church" better than any other woman, except perhaps, Margaret Blaarer. For the wives of the other leading reformers, as Anna Zwingli and Anna Bullinger, lived quiet lives or busied themselves mainly with their household duties. Idelette Calvin is almost unknown, because she is hidden behind her great husband. But Catharine Zell stands out prominently, both by her life and writings. She seems to have been the equal of her husband in ability, and had even greater energy. While she excelled in the management of her home and made it a delightful refuge for all suffering refugees, yet with her pen she defended her opinions also. Her defence of the Reformed against the Lutherans endears her to all women of the Reformed Church. She was a female theologian in the best sense of that word, a true Reformed, a warm-hearted woman, and a pious Christian.

II.

MARGARET BLAARER.

NOT only were the wives of the reformers a great aid to the Reformation, but their sisters also. We have an illustration of this in Margaret Blaarer the sister of Ambrose Blaarer, the great reformer of Constance and Wurtemberg. In this city Huss had been burned at the stake prophesying that the Reformation would rise from his ashes. In 1527 that city rose, Phœnixlike, from his ashes to throw off the yoke of Rome; as many as twenty-three ministers preaching the gospel in the churches, out of which the Catholic images and altars had been cast. The Catholic priests and bishops fled from the city. In this Reformation the the Blaarer family became very prominent. Ambrose, the reformer, had been a monk, but left the monastery disgusted with its vices. His brother Thomas became burgomaster of the town and Margaret became the female reformer of the Swiss Reformation.

Many, however, were the difficulties that arose to impede the Reformation there. Drought, plague and earthquake came one after the other. During all these trials Margaret was the excellent helper of her brother Ambrose. She was a scholar in those days, when few women were educated. She read the old authors in the original tongues, had correspondence with many learned men in Latin and was highly honored as a poetess by Erasmus and Bullinger. Bucer, the reformer of Strasburg, having attended the conference at Berne in 1528, returned with Blaarer to Germany by way of Constance. He there learned to know Ambrose's sister, and afterwards kept up correspondence with her, no less than seventy-nine letters of Bucer to her being shown in the Zurich library. He addressed her as "sister" and "mother," although he was three years older than she. But then she was a mother in Israel because of her good works. But it was her piety that shone above all her gifts. For though so honored by men, and so well acquainted with the sciences of the day, she clothed herself, says a writer, "in the greater ornament of modesty, that she had not only found the pearl of great price, but was a pearl herself (Margaret means pearl) through the splendor of her piety and her example of good works." And not only this but also an ornament to her city.

In doing good she was untiring. Many were the

poor children she taught to read. Many were the widows and orphans she visited in their sorrow. While her brother Ambrose swung the spiritual sword, the Word of God, and her other brother Thomas swung the worldly sword as a leader of the Reformation in the city council, her work was the quiet, still labor of a love that reached all. The first woman's society to care for the sick was organized by her. She thus became the founder of the first woman's society in the Protestant Church. When the plague broke ont in 1541 she labored most assiduously and self-denyingly among the sick at the risk of her own life. Her brother Ambrose thus wrote to Bullinger November 5, 1541, "Margaret, the best of sisters, behaves like an archdeaconess of our church in that she puts her life and all in danger. Daily she visits the houses where the patients of the pest are cared for. She has just taken a little girl whom she has supported for ten years, into her home. Pray, I beseech you, to the Lord, that He does not permit her who is our only comfort to be torn away from us."

Ambrose's wish was answered. She did not die of the plague, but she did not live long after; for she died of a fever, November 15, 1541, at the age of 47 years. After her death, Ambrose received many letters full of sympathy and mourning from all the leading reformers as Bucer and Bullinger. Ambrose wrote a beautiful hymn on her death, full of Christian hope; for he was one of the earliest hymn-writers of the Reformed, as for 150 years after the Reformation they sang mainly psalms.

She was a genuine sister of mercy, not one shut up in a convent, but one who entered the far wider sphere of everyday life, busy in acts of mercy wherever opportunity was found. If her brother has been called the Apostle of Wurtemberg, she might well be called the Angel of Mercy of Constance.

Well was it for her that she died when she did. It was a mercy of God that she did not live a few years longer, for then she would have seen the Reformed driven out of Constance and her brother Ambrose compelled to flee to Switzerland for safety. When that storm burst on Constance, she was safe above all storms in the bosom of her Lord in heaven.

Chapter III.—FRANCE.

I.

QUEEN MARGARET OF NAVARRE.

THE first princess to become Reformed was Queen Margaret of Navarre. Before any other lady of royal blood became Reformed, she did. The Reformed doctrines already at their beginning reached up to a throne and as in Paul's time there were saints found in Cæsar's household. Margaret was a remarkable combination of qualities. She was one of the most beautiful princesses of her day, and learned as well. The statesmen of her time considered her the best head in Europe. But above all her beauty and ability shone her piety. Her beauty of soul was greater than her beauty of body. To her the Reformed of France owed everything, for had it not been for her influence and protection, they would have been crushed out at the very beginning.

She was born April 11, 1492, at Angouleme. While she was yet a girl, there was a Frenchman preaching the Gospel before the time of the Reformation. His name was Lefevre, and he preached it as early as 1512 (four years before Zwingli and five years before Luther). He taught that Christ saves, and not the Church, for the Church must herself be purified. His preaching and the letters of Bishop Briconnet won Margaret, when young, to the Evangelical faith, although she still remained a member of the Romish Church, as the Protestants had not yet formally separated from that Church. She had one brother, who became Francis I., King of France. He cared nothing for the Reformed faith (for his sympathies were with the Romish party), but he cared much for his sister. When an enemy complained to him that Margaret was inclining to Protestantism, he replied, "If what you say is true, I love her too well to allow her to be troubled on that account." Often he said in the presence of her enemies, "My sister Margaret is the only woman I ever knew who had every virtue and every grace without any admixture of vice." Thus in the corrupt court of Louisa of Savoy she preached Christ with wonderful sweetness, and influenced many of the nobility to become Reformed. Her influence over her brother she utilized to spread and to protect Protestantism. She hoped that he would put himself at the head of the Protestants, as Emperor Charles V. of Spain had done at the head of the Romanists. She tried in every way to introduce Protestant influences at court. A German nobleman, the Count of Hohenloe, who was a great friend of hers, became a Protestant. As he was a high dignitary in the Romish Church, he had great influence; and as he spoke French as readily as German, he hoped to win France for the Reformation. Queen Margaret was the door through which he hoped it might enter France. So he composed a book entitled "The Book of the Cross," which he hoped would influence her. When her brother, Francis, returned from Spain, Margaret hoped to influence him, so that he would gather around her the friends of the Gospel, and so wrote to Hohenloe. She hoped that Francis would invite Hohenloe to Paris, that he might gain an opportunity to preach the Gospel. But Francis, on his return, to her great surprise and sorrow, forbade Protestant books, and was careful never to invite Hohenloe. All that Margaret could do to console herself was to write some of her beautiful religious poems, as:

> O Thou my Priest, my Advocate, my King,
> On whom depends my life, my everything;
> O Lord, who first didst drain the bitter cup of woe,
> And knowest its poison (if man e'er did know),

These thorns how sharp, these wounds how deep—
Saviour, Friend, King, oh, plead my cause, I pray;
Speak, help, and save me, lest I fall away.

In 1533 she published a volume of religious poems entitled "The Mirror of the Sinful Soul"—a commentary on the words "Create in me a clean heart, O Lord." In it she dwells on the great sacrifice of Christ for sin and never mentions the Catholic doctrines of the intercession of saints, human merit or purgatory. This omission gave great offence to the Catholics. She is therefore the first great female poetess of the Reformed. The Reformed rejoiced in this defence of their principles by no less a person than the Queen; but the Catholics were so incensed that some of their students acted an allegorical play in which she was held up to ridicule. Her religious poems reveal great beauty and ability, all sanctified by her great piety.

When she found she could no longer use her influence to introduce Protestantism, she used it to protect it, especially after the persecutions of the Reformed had begun. During the persecutions, whenever she was in Paris, her brother, out of respect to her, would not allow any Protestants to be put to death. The Romanists plotted against her, but her learning, piety and benevolence, as well as her genius and beauty, providentially prevented them from hurting her. Again and again she protected the Reformed, and often saved their lives. Thus a young man of rare qualities, one of her friends at the university, was, during her absence from Paris, arrested, dragged through the streets of the city, followed by a howling mob, and thrust into prison. The cell into which he was placed, was a damp and loathesome place. There was no floor where he could sit down, and only one place (the cell being partly filled with water) where he could stand or crouch with his back against the damp stone wall. Here he was kept without light, air or attention, except when given food, for three days, until he was utterly exhausted. At last the cell door was opened, and he found himself released. He knew in his heart that Margaret had done this. But when, with his torn and filthy garments, he went, staggering from weakness and lack of food, through the streets of Paris, not even his old friends would speak to him or answer his appeal for food. Alas, his persecution had closed their hearts against him. He determined to go to the palace and appeal to his deliverer. Standing like a beggar at the gate, which he had so often entered with honor, he wrote a note to her, stating his sad condition. She immediately ordered him into her presence. When he reached her elegant drawing room, he found her, in all her resplendent beauty and magnificence, surrounded by ambassadors and cardinals. As soon as he entered, she advanced to meet him, introduced him to all her company, and then sent him to an apartment, where everything was done for his comfort. So noble and fearless she showed herself in the face of persecution. It seems that as soon as she had returned to the city during his imprisonment, she had gone to her brother and with tears begged for his release, as he was an innocent man; and Francis granted it, for he never could refuse her. The Romanists only hated her the more for this act, and caricatured her in a play as a witch riding on a broomstick, an insult which her brother was very prompt to resent, and it was stopped.

Marot, her valet de chambre and the best poet of his age, was arrested. He spent his time writing poems in prison, and soon Margaret had him free, too. It would have been a great loss to the French Reformed Church, if she had not accomplished this, for he was the author of the French translation of the Psalms, which were sung in that Church for the last three centuries.

Berquin, one of the most learned of the French nobles, her special friend, was also arrested (1523) for his evangelical ideas, but released through her influence. Two years after, Berquin was again arrested and severely examined by the Sorbonne. When they urged him to recant just a little and observe some Romish rite, so as to save his life, he replied, "I will not yield a single point." He expected to be burned at the stake, but lo! again Margaret gained liberty for him in 1526. But in 1529 Berquin, who aimed to rescue France from the pope, was again arrested and imprisoned. Margaret again used all her efforts to have him released, but all in vain, and to her great sorrow Berquin was put to death, April 22, 1529, as a martyr for the Reformed faith.

When the reformers, like Lefevre and Roussel, had fled from France and gathered at Strasburg, she undertook to bring them all back. She went to her brother, who was generally ready to grant her everything. He allowed them to return, and the reformers hastened back to thank her for her influence. She continued influencing her brother, until in 1534, wonderful to relate, he allowed Roussel to preach in the leading church of Paris, the Notre Dame church, but the people would not permit it. She was also helpful in getting her brother to invite Melanchthon to come to France.

In 1527 occurred her second marriage which was with the King Henry of Navarre. Splendid was the wedding, but she found that her married life was not all bliss, and her pious mind went upward to a better marriage as she wrote:

> Would that the day were come, O Lord,
> So much desired by me,
> When by the cords of heavenly love
> I shall be drawn to Thee,
> United in eternal life
> The husband Thou and I the wife.
>
> That wedding day, O Lord,
> My heart so longs to see,
> That neither fame nor wealth nor rank
> Can give to me;
> To me the world no more
> Can yield delight;
> Unless Thou, Lord, be with me here,
> Lo! all is dark as night.

The kingdom of her husband had never been entered by the doctrines of the Reformation. She at once began spreading them by her example and influence. Her husband as a Romanist was not pleased with this, but said nothing to oppose her, except on one occasion. Margaret usually had private Evangelical service in her apartments, when Lefevre or Roussel would preach, and one day she observed the communion. There was an underground hall in her palace called the "Mint," beneath the terrace of the castle. Here her servants privately placed a table, covered it with a white cloth, and placed on it a plate of bread and cups of wine. Margaret went there and joined with the Protestants in their communion service. But though it was done secretly, the news of it got abroad and came to the ears of the king, who was very much annoyed at what he called "the fastings in the cellar." One day as he returned from hunting, he asked where she was. And when told that she was in her apartments, listening to a preacher, he went to them. The minister and the others being warned, succeeded in escaping, and Margaret, trembling and anxious, was there alone to receive him. The king flushed with anger, struck her in the face, saying, "Madame, you know too much." This was too great an insult to be passed over lightly. She reported it to her brother. That any one should lay violent hands on his beautiful and idolized sister, was too much for Francis, and he at once set out for Navarre, threatening war. The news of his coming filled the king of Navarre with fear. He begged his wife to forgive him, and he became so penitent that he not only promised to allow Reformed worship, but even promised to investigate the Reformed doctrines. This incident led to the conversion of the king himself, and so the Reformed faith was introduced into Navarre, and that land became an asylum for the Reformed fleeing from France.

Margaret invited to her palace at Nerac, the leading Huguenots, when driven out of France. At her table they would discuss passages of Scripture, with the Queen as a delighted listener, who often took part in the discussions. A beautiful illustration is told of the last day of Lefevre's life, that while the rest of the company were enjoying their meal, Lefevre appeared very sad. With difficulty she succeeded in getting from him the cause. He said that he must die soon, and face his Maker; and though he had lived a pure life, yet, while many who had fol-

QUEEN MARGARET ENTERTAINING FRENCH REFUGEES AT NERAC

lowed the Evangelical teachings had boldly come out for Protestantism and even died for it; he, by flight from persecution, had never taken his stand by publicly leaving the Romish church. The Queen comforted him and he appeared satisfied. He then appointed her his executrix. And when she asked what she would have to do, he replied, "The task of distributing my effects to the poor." She replied, "I accept the trust and it is more acceptable to me than if my brother had left me the whole kingdom of France." Lefevre then laid down to sleep, and in sleeping passed away.

Just before she died, it is said, she conformed to Catholic usages, but her correspondence at that time was so evangelical as to exasperate the Catholics. She died December 21, 1548, rejoicing in hope. In dying she called on Jesus, and not the Virgin, to save her. "God," she said, "I am assured, will carry forward the work He has permitted me to commence, and my place will be more than filled by my daughter, who has the energy and moral courage, in which, I fear, I have been deficient." Her dying hope was grandly fulfilled in her daughter, Jeanne d'Albret, who bravely fought the battles for the Reformed, and in her grandson, Henry, who became king of France and gave to the Reformed the Edict of Nantes, which gave them liberty to worship in France.

II.

QUEEN JEANNE D'ALBRET OF NAVARRE.

A PROTESTANT Joan of Arc was this noble lady. She was the daughter of Queen Margaret of Navarre. But she was greater than her mother in moral courage. Her mother merely began the Reformation, but Jeanne was its greatest military female defender. She was born at the palace at Fontainbleau, January 7, 1528. She was an open, frank, fearless girl—the very soul of truth. She was reared in France, away from her father and mother (who lived in Navarre,) because the king of France wanted to retain control over her. She was surrounded by Romish influences, in fact was not given the chance to be a Protestant while she was a girl. But the king of France soon found that she had a will of her own. Before she was three months old, the king of Spain had asked for her hand for his son; and when she was about fourteen years old, the king of France determined to marry her, a mere girl, to a German prince, the duke of Cleve, in a political marriage. The king was very much surprised when he found that Jeanne absolutely refused to marry the duke. The king had her father and mother help him, but all their influences, and even threats (as, that she would be whipped to death), were of no avail with her. The king was inexorable, she must marry. So she did what she could. She drew up two protests against the marriage, stating that she was forced into it against her will. These were witnessed and filed, and became of use afterwards, as we shall see. Still she was forced (1546) to the wedding ceremony. But so unwilling was she that they had to carry her to the altar—an unwilling bride. The duke then went to war and she was permitted to go home with her mother; and then for the first time she came into contact with the Reformed faith. As the duke of Cleve soon after turned against the king of France, her marriage with him was annulled by the pope on account of the protests she had filed.

When she became twenty years old, her beauty again attracted suitors. She is described as fair, with a generous, open countenance and violet eyes. Among her suitors was the Bourbon prince, Antoine, duke of Vendome. Him she accepted for her husband. When her father died, the king of France wanted to appropriate to himself her little mountain kingdom of Navarre; but now for the first time Jeanne revealed her watchfulness and ability as a stateswoman. She raised troops and prepared for war. Fortunately, just as she was in danger of being destroyed, the king of France died, and her land was delivered from danger. Then she made an open profession of the Reformed faith before her people and the world at Pau, her capital, December 5, 1560. Still France and the Romanists were not idle. Catharine de Medici, her bitter enemy, one of the most deceitful of women—the Jezebel of her age—plotted against her.. She concocted a plan to separate Jeanne's husband from her, win him back to the Romish faith, and thus gain the kingdom of Navarre to France. As Antoine was then regent of France, and had to be in France, away from Jeanne, a large part of his time, there was danger that this foul plan would be carried out. Alas for Jeanne! her husband was caught in the toils of the enemy and soon went back to the Catholic faith. And when afterwards Jeanne visited Paris, he treated her with contempt and tried to force her to go to mass. But she would not be forced against her conscience. When Catharine de Medici now aided her husband in trying to make her give up her Reformed faith, she nobly replied to her (although she was brokenhearted at the time by the infidelity of her husband),

"Madam, if I at this moment held my son and all the kingdoms of the world in my grasp, I would hurl them into the bottom of the sea, rather than peril the salvation of my soul." Her enemies even went so far as to plot against her life; one of them even urging that she be thrown over the wall into the river Seine. Seeing her danger, she asked to be permitted to leave France. Permission was given her, but it was given treacherously, for plans were laid to murder her on the way home. As she parted from her son, the parting was heart-rending. She trembled to leave him behind with the Romanists and the French, and yet they would not permit him to go with her. In leaving him she made him promise never to go to mass, which he, bursting into tears, agreed to.

To regain authority over her own land of Navarre she with great boldness and matchless adroitness led her little company of 200 through a land full of enemies, all the while receiving recruits from the people as she passed. She did not know all the dangers that threatened her. But the Reformed duke of Conde garrisoned Vendome, where she was to spend the night, and thus prevented her enemies from murdering her. The next day Montluc, who was sent in pursuit of her, followed her so closely that her flight was a race for her life. She sent ahead swift couriers to summon her soldiers to her aid. Her enemies were almost on her—so close that the blast of their trumpets could be heard by her retinue—when, lo, eight hundred of her brave soldiers from Navarre swooped down on her party, and took them under their protection and saved her. It was the first of her many hair-breadth escapes, but it was not the last. It, however, roused all the womanhood that was in her. She now realized her danger and their treachery. With sublime courage, marvellous military skill and dexterous celerity she dealt a blow at her enemies before they were ready to meet her armies. Her husband threatened her for introducing Protestantism into her land, but it mattered not to her. A little while after he was called to meet his death. The face of his wronged wife seemed to come up before him as he was filled with remorse. It is said that he again professed the Reformed faith before he died, and vowed that if he were permitted to live, he would introduce it everywhere in France. As owing to his death she now had greater power, Jeanne issued her order abolishing the Romish religion in Navarre, because she found that her Romish subjects were always plotting against her. When the Pope in return issued a bull against her, she with rare diplomacy compelled him to recall it by making even her arch enemy, Catharine de Medici, her intercessor with the Pope. And when the Pope talked of disinheriting her family by declaring her marriage with Antoine void, because she had been married before to the duke of Cleve, she then with marvellous diplomacy compelled Catharine again to prevent the Pope from doing it, as that would not only disinherit her son and keep him from the throne of France, but would put on the throne the prince of Conde, whom Catharine hated worse than she did Jeanne's son. Marvellous was her skill in making even her enemies do her work. In it all a kind providence seemed to continually watch over her. For when the king of Spain started a rebellion in her land, that he might draw her to it and then capture her, lo! the king's own wife warned Jeanne of this plot, and she was saved, for she seemed to have a charmed life.

Finally King Charles IX. of France and the king of Spain together plotted to massacre all the Reformed, but especially Jeanne and the prince of

Conde. Without a moment's delay she gathered the forces of her little mountain land. This prevented the massacre, or at least postponed it for eight years, till the awful day of St. Bartholomew. She now had one great desire, and that was to see her son, then thirteen years of age. Her great purpose was to get him out of France and under her control. She was afraid he might become a Catholic, or worse than that, in the immoral French court. When she again visited France, she succeeded in gaining permission for her boy to accompany her as far as Vendome. Swiftly she planned his escape. But one mistake and all would have been fatal. She secretly sent a messenger to her own court, telling them to have an armed force to meet her. Six hours after this courier left, at midnight, she and her son stole away and galloped at the highest speed for Pau, her capital, and arrived there safely, though it was a hot flight. She now had her son under her control, and carefully did she have him trained under her eye. He soon revealed remarkable abilities, especially in the art of war. He was being prepared by providence for his part in the next great war between the Huguenots and Catholics. Into this conflict Jeanne threw all her fortunes. Although her mountain kingdom of Navarre (situated southwest of France and between France and Spain) was not involved in this war, for it was a combat between the two religions in France; yet she foresaw that the defeat of the Reformed in France meant the downfall of her kingdom, too, because it was Reformed.

So just as Gustavus Adolphus left Sweden to save Protestantism in Germany, she went to the salvation of the Huguenots of France. Her courage rose to a sublime height, and she threw the fortunes of herself and her son into this war for the Reformed. She was afraid to tell this decision of her heart to her own counsellors at Navarre, for fear they would prevent her from carrying it out. So she stole away secretly from her own land and arrived at Rochelle, where the Huguenots of France had gathered for their defence. Her arrival astounded that city. The Reformed were beside themselves with joy at this new and unexpected reinforcement. The mayor of the city presented her with the keys to the city. She was greeted with thunders of applause as she first entered the council of the Huguenots. There the prince of Conde, their idol and leader, arose and resigned his command of the Huguenot army into the hands of Jeanne's son, Henry. The audience responded enthusiastically to this. Then it was that she arose, and with beauty and dignity declined the offer. "No, gentlemen," she said, "I and my children are here to promote the success of this great cause or to share in its disaster. The cause of God is dearer to me than the aggrandizement of my son." After her address she compelled her son to decline the honor of commander-in-chief amid such applause as showed they would accept Henry as their leader, although he was only sixteen years old at the time. When the Huguenots found that she would not allow her son to lead their forces, they placed her at the head of the civil government, as the governess of Rochelle. Many were her cares, yet in the midst of them all she had the New Testament translated into the Basque language for a part of her subjects and published at her own expense. She had charge of all the correspondence with foreign princes, and it was her pleadings that secured Queen Elizabeth of England for an ally to the Huguenots. Queen Elizabeth is rated as a greater woman in history than Jeanne, but in character she does not begin to touch her. She was profane, where Jeanne was pure. She was selfish and whimsical, where Jeanne was frank and unselfish. Elizabeth lived for herself, Jeanne for the Reformed. But Elizabeth helped her to save the Huguenots by aiding Rochelle with her fleet. Terrible was that war, but Jeanne rose above all its misfortunes and cares. The king of Spain and the king of France now determined that while Jeanne was away from her kingdom at Rochelle, they would seize her kingdom, but she had it defended and saved. Then came the death of the prince of Conde, March 13, 1569, the idolized military leader of the Huguenots. This so paralyzed the Huguenot army that not even Coligny could rally their courage. Despairing, Coligny sent for her to come to camp, and told her she was the only one who had influence enough to inspire the army again with enthusiasm and courage, so as to march on to victory. She came before the army with its flags draped in mourning for Conde, and their hearts hid in gloom. By her side rode the son of the dead Conde, while on the other side rode her son, Henry. Then she made her great address, saying, "Soldiers, you weep. But does the memory of Conde demand nothing but profitless tears? No, let us unite and summon back our courage to defend a cause

JEANNE D'ALBRET ADDRESSING THE HUGUENOT ARMY

which can never perish and to avenge him who was its firm support. Does despair overwhelm you—despair, that shameful feeling of weak natures? When I, the queen, hope still, is it for you to fear? Because Conde is dead, is all therefore lost? Does our cause cease to be just and holy? No; God, who had already rescued you from perils innumerable, has raised up brothers-in-arms worthy to succeed Conde. To these leaders I add my own son. Make proof of his valor. The blood of Bourbon and Valois flows in his veins. He burns with ardor to avenge the death of the prince. Behold also Conde's son, the worthy inheritor of his father's virtues. He succeeded to his name and to his glory. Soldiers, I offer to you everything in my power to bestow—my dominions, my treasures, my life, and that which is dearer to me than all, my children. I make here a solemn oath before you all—and you know me too well to doubt my word—I swear to defend to my last sigh the holy cause which now unites us, which is that of honor and truth." When she ceased, there was a breathless silence for a moment, and then everywhere wild shouts went up along the lines, and as if seized by a sudden impulse, the army hailed the young prince Henry as their leader.

Thus she stood there before her army, a greater than Joan of Arc, inspiring her army not by the sword, but by the subtle power of her matchless character. This was the grandest scene of many in her life. With wonderful tact she, with Coligny, conducted the war. But her beloved Coligny was defeated and badly wounded at Moncontour. She at once set off to see him, though great dangers threatened her way. She found him in bed with his jaw so badly shattered that he could not speak. But though he could not speak, he could weep tears of thankfulness for her coming. Forgetting that defeat, she at once planned for victory. Everywhere the white plume of her son was waving to victory, until the Huguenot army encamped under the very walls of Paris and forced the Catholics to make peace. Then she returned, covered with victories, amid the applause of the people, to her kingdom of Navarre.

But, alas! now the Romanists determined to conquer by diplomacy and deceit, where they could not conquer by war. They laid the plans for what ultimately culminated in the awful massacre of St.

Bartholomew. Jeanne, with her wonderful insight, foresaw that there was deception, but she could not tell exactly into what danger it would lead. But Coligny was confidingly led into the trap. Its first step was to get young Henry of Navarre to marry the daughter of the king of France. Jeanne objected. She did not want her son to marry a Catholic, for fear of their influence. But all her councillors, with Coligny at their head, forced her to consent to the marriage. The Romanists were so anxious to bring it about, that they even agreed that the marriage should be according to the Reformed form. Finally Jeanne, forced by all around to give her consent, went to Paris to make the necessary contracts, and to see that the rights of her land and of her religion were preserved. She opposed the French on many points, but they agreed to all, and she finally signed the articles of marriage. But still she was not satisfied. She felt there was deception somewhere. St. Bartholomew's massacre "seemed to cast its shadow before" upon her. She did not know what was coming; she only felt it would be an injury to the Reformed. Her anxieties proved too much for her. She was taken sick before the wedding, on June 4, 1572. The Huguenots were dismayed by her sickness. If she died, who would look after them, for she had been so long their patron saint? But her faith was triumphant at her death, as she said, "I have never feared death. I do not dare to murmur at the will of God, but I grieve deeply to leave my children exposed to so many dangers. Still I trust it all to Him." She died, June 9, 1572, in her Reformed faith, with her Bible at her side, relying on its promises and receiving its crown. One of her last acts was to enjoin her son to remain true to the Reformed religion.

Thus died the Deborah of the Reformed Church of France. Just as Landgravine Amalie Elizabeth, of Hesse Cassel, was the Deborah of the Reformed of Germany, so was she to France. She had unfurled her banners in the name of the Lord and of her Reformed faith. She has taken a front rank among the military leaders of those Reformation times. When her generals were killed, captured or wounded, she rallied her troops, inspired them with courage and guided them to victory. In all her wars she never had been conquered. And yet she did not do it for herself, but for her Reformed faith. She has came down to us as one of the most beautiful brilliant and strongest female characters of history.

But she died not a moment too soon. She had seen great sorrows, but a greater one was to come after her death, the awful massacre of St. Bartholomew, which would have broken her heart, even if it should not have taken her life. Perhaps, had she lived, she, with her wonderful divination of character, might have discovered it in time to prevent it, or with her wonderful fertility of resources might have been enabled to combat it. At least it is an open question of history whether it would have happened had she lived. But she was gone. She died while her cause was yet glorious before defeat and massacre came. So died the woman who combined the Deborah of the Bible and the Joan of Arc in history in one character. She could sing with Deborah, "So let all thine enemies perish, but let them that love thee be as the sun when he goeth forth in his might."

III.

CHARLOTTE D'MORNAY.

CHARLOTTE ARBALESTE, who later became the wife of the celebrated Philip De Mornay, the famous French statesman, was born February, 1549. Although her mother remained a Catholic till her death, her father became a Protestant in the later years of his life. Many years before, while traveling through Germany, he came into contact with Protestantism, and at Strasburg heard a theological discussion between the Reformed and the Romanists which opened his eyes to some of the abuses of the latter. But he remained ignorant of Evangelical truth for many years, until being charged by the Romanists with being a heretic, he determined to examine into the Huguenot heresy and finally accepted it. His last words in dying, 1570, were, "Lord, thou gavest me a soul fifty-eight years ago; thou gavest it me white and clean. I render it to thee impure and polluted. Wash it in the blood of Jesus Christ, thy son."

Charlotte was married September 28, 1567, to the Seigneur de Feuqueres, a brave and zealous Huguenot, who died of a fever about two years later.

His death left her in financial straits, but the Lord raised up friends, and later she went to Paris to receive her share in her father's inheritance. It thus happened that she was in Paris at the awful massacre of St. Bartholomew and was saved only by a providence. She says that at first she was not alarmed; but when she saw companies of soldiers, each wearing a white cross on his hat going about the street, she felt there was danger. But as there was so much danger in the streets she remained in her apartments. She then sent her maidservant and little daughter to a Catholic friend, who sent word back that Charlotte would also be welcome if she would come. She had hardly left her apartments when the soldiers burst in and were greatly angered that she could not be found. The number of refugees in this friend's house increased to forty, but they remained until the third day, Tuesday evening. Then suspicion was aroused, the house being ordered to be searched. Warning of this having come, all escaped except Charlotte and another. She with her maid, was put in an empty loft, while her child was sent in safety to her Catholic grandmother. Then she was hidden in the houses of several friends for three lays more, and finally taken to a corn-merchant's. Her mother then tried to get her to go to mass, if only to simply save her life. But she absolutely refused. Her Reformed faith was dearer to her than her own life.

At length, after being there five days she determined to leave Paris by all hazards. Her chamber there was immediately above that of a Catholic lady and she did not dare walk in her room for fear of being discovered. She did not dare light a candle lest the suspicions of the neighbors should be excited. When anything was brought her, it was only a morsel, secretly. So on Wednesday, the eleventh day of the massacre, she succeeded in getting into a boat on the Seine to go to Sens. At Tournelles a guard demanded her passport. As she had none he charged her with being a Huguenot. In despair almost, she asked to be taken to a gentleman there, with whom her grandmother who was a Catholic had had business. Two soldiers brought her to the gate. Her friends assured the soldiers that she was a good Catholic, and she was taken back to the boat and permitted to go on her journey. But she was still in the greatest danger, yet the Lord delivered her safely. For at the moment she was arrested at the boat, the house of the corn-merchant where she had been was searched and she would have been killed had she been found there.

She traveled to Villegrand where for fifteen days she found an asylum in the country with a vinedresser. She then went to Sedan where she found safety for the duke of Bouillon, its ruler, was a member of the Reformed faith. There she remained and while there she met her second husband, Philip DeMornay, one of the most devoted Huguenots, who like herself had almost miraculously escaped St. Bartholomew's massacre. He was distinguished as a Christian, a statesman, a soldier, and an author. They were married January 3, 1576. He was sent as an ambassador to England and Holland and she traveled with him. They returned to Paris in July, 1582, and went from there to Montauban in southern France, where she lived.

While there, a peculiar case of church discipline occurred in the Reformed church. The consistory of that congregation were quite rigid about simplicity of dress, holding it to be unbecoming for Christian woman to wear curls, and they prohibited it under pain of exclusion from the Lord's Supper. They quoted 1 Timothy 2:10-11, "In like manner also that women adorn themselves in modest apparel, with shamefacedness and sobriety; not with braided hair of gold or pearls, but (which becometh women professing godliness) with good works"; and also 1 Peter 3, "Whose adorning, let it not be that outward adorning, of plaiting of the hair and of wearing of gold or of putting on of apparel, but let it be the hidden man of the heart, in that which is not corruptible, even the ornament of a meek and quiet spirit, which in the sight of God is of great price." Charlotte and her daughters not obeying this injunction of the consistory, were prohibited from coming to the Lord's Supper by the consistory. DeMornay, her husband, severely reprimanded the consistory, but it was all in vain. She replied to the consistory saying that the Reformed church nowhere else acted in this manner, and that 1 Timothy 2:9, as Calvin showed in his commentary, referred more to the reformation of manners than to dress. She finally appealed from the consistory to the General Synod of the Reformed Church of France. We are not informed how the matter was finally adjusted there, but part of her family began attending the Lord's Supper in a neighboring Reformed congregation, and she in 1589 removed to Saumur. There, when her husband, being relieved of active service by the king, returned, he found her building at her own expense a church for the Reformed congregation. This was dedicated a few days after his return.

Her heart seemed bound up in the life of her only son Philip, to whom, when he was in Holland, she wrote a most beautiful motherly letter. "My son, God is my witness that even before your birth, He inspired me with a hope that you would serve Him; and this to you ought to be some pledge of His grace and an admonition to perform your duty. Your father and I have also taken care to instruct you in every branch of useful learning, to the end that you may not only live, but also shine in His church. You are young, my son, and divers imaginations present themselves to youth, but always remember the saying of the Psalmist, 'How shall a young man direct his way? Certainly by conducting himself according to thy word, O Lord.' Nor will there be wanting persons who will desire to turn you aside therefrom to the left hand or the right. But say also with the Psalmist, 'I will associate only with those that keep thy laws. Thy laws, O God, shall be the men of my counsel.'" Beautiful words, and nobly he fulfilled them, for he grew up a beautiful Christian character in answer to such prayers and admonitions.

His death, in battle, in 1605, while fighting for the Dutch, almost broke her heart. She never recovered from the shock, and survived him only a few months. On Sunday, May 7th, 1606, she attended morning service at the church and expected to go in the afternoon to catechising, but she became ill. She endured great suffering until the following Sunday, when her husband broke the news to her, that she must die. She received the news with joy. She bore her dying testimony, saying, "I am going to God, persuaded that nothing can separate me from His love. I know that my Redeemer liveth. He has triumphed." One of her physicians, a Catholic, exhorted her to take courage. She replied, "My courage is from above." She then spoke to him of the superior consolation that the Protestant religion offered over the Catholic, and urged him to look to Christ and him crucified. The next day her pastor recalled to her Christ's words, "Father, into thy hand I commend my spirit." She added the additional words of the 31st Psalm, "For thou hast redeemed me, O eternal God of truth." She expired with the word "Jesus" on her lips, May

15, 1606. Her husband bore a beautiful tribute to her memory when he said of her, "She assisted me to live well, and by her pious death, she has taught me how to die well."

IV.
PHILLIPINE DE LUNS.

A MARTYR woman was this Reformed saint, for the female sex furnished its quota of martyrs for our faith. She was born at Gascogne, France. Of her youth we know nothing. At an early age she was married to a noble gentleman named Von Graberon. She went with him to Paris, so as to join the Reformed church there, of which he was an elder. Often the Huguenots would assemble themselves in her house, and the neighbors would hear them singing psalms, as they were not allowed to have a church in the city. But soon her husband died, and in 1557 she was left a widow at the early age of 23. Soon after her husband's death, September 4, 1557, she met with four hundred French Reformed in a hall in the street of St. Jacques behind the university. There they celebrated the Lord's Supper, and the minister preached on the words of institution in First Corinthians, eleventh chapter. But at midnight, as they wanted to go home, they heard terrible noises outside. The mob evidently wanted to burst in the doors; for the fanatical people believed that these Huguenots had been the cause of the defeat of the

French army at St. Quentin, and they had gathered large quantities of stones to throw at them as they came out of the Reformed service.

While the enemy were making outcries without the house, the Reformed within became greatly frightened. The elders urged them to become quiet, and then asked them whether they would choose to stay there until the light of the morning would make it safer for them to go home, or whether they desired to fight their way that night through the armed crowd outside, and thus escape. Many men reached for their daggers and determined to force their way out, and thus many escaped. But many others, among them Phillipine, had to remain behind. And when the day dawned, they were arrested. As they were led forth, the crowd fell upon them and abused them fearfully. With clothing torn into shreds and full of the mud thrown on them, they were led to prison. In this terrible prison Phillipine remained a whole year. Often she was heard singing the twenty-fifth and the forty-second psalms. Priests often came to her to try to bring her back to the Catholic faith, but she always came out victor in their attacks. Once one of them asked her: "Do you believe that the wafer at the communion is the true body of our Lord?" She replied: "How could He, who filled heaven and earth, be contained in a piece of bread, which mice could eat and cobwebs pollute?" Her testimony for Evangelical truth was so firm that they put her into closer confinement. Heretofore she had been permitted to see her sister, but after this she was sentenced to solitary confinement.

From this time the course of the law was hastened for the Romanists found there was no hope of converting her back to Rome. And besides, the judge wanted to convict her, so as to get a share in her estates. Meanwhile Calvin from Geneva was urging the Protestant princes of Germany to use their influence with the French, so that these prisoners might be spared. But their intercession came too late. She was brought before her judges for trial. Her ordeal was quite severe, but her answers were based on the Bible. She was asked: "Do you believe in the mass?" She replied: "About this sacrament I will believe only what is found in the Old and New Testaments. I have not yet found there that the mass is from God." "Will you receive the wafer?" "No; I will receive only what Christ has sealed." "How long is it since you confessed to the priest?" "I do not remember, but I do know that I have daily made confession to my Lord. Other confession is not commanded by Christ, for He alone has the power to forgive sin." "What do you believe about prayer to the Virgin and to the saints?" "I know no other prayer than that which our Lord taught to His disciples. To Him we must go, and to no other. The saints in paradise are happy, that I know, but pray to them I will not." "Do you observe fasting on Friday and Sunday?" "No; because it is not commanded in the Bible." They then tried to argue with her about it by saying "that the Church required fasting, and even if non-fasting were not sinful in itself, it would become sinful because the Church forbade it." Very ably she replied: "I do not believe in any other commandment than that Christ gave. And nowhere in the New Testament do I find that power is given to the pope to rule the Church." But they argued, "the spiritual and worldly powers are ordained of God, and should be obeyed." She answered: "The Church has no other authority in it than that of Christ." "Who taught you this?" "The Old and New Testaments." Like her Saviour at His temptations, she answered them out of the Word of God.

On September 27, 1558, she was sentenced to death. An old man, Clivet, and a young man, Gravelle, both elders of the Reformed Church, who had been arrested at the same time that she had, were sentenced to die with her. All three were tortured severely, and after torture they were thrown into the chapel of the courthouse. There they waited for their deliverance from this imprisonment of earth to the freedom of heaven. As usual, the priest came to try to convert them back to Catholicism before they died, but the priest's efforts were all useless. They laid aside their garments of sorrow and put on their best clothing, because they said they were going not to a funeral, but to a wedding, and they wanted to be ready to meet their bridegroom, the Lord Jesus Christ. They were then placed on wagons and taken to the place of execution. Clivet, who had been a schoolmaster in the country districts, and whose picture had once been burned by the Romanists, bore his Christian testimony boldly to the bystanders as the wagon rode along. A priest said to Phillipine that she should confess to him. She replied: "I continually confess in my heart to my Lord and am certain of the forgiveness of sin." Some of the councillors bade her take a wooden cross in her hand, saying as an argument that Christ had bade men to carry the cross. She, however, refused in the least to do any homage to Rome, but replied that Christ indeed bade us bear the cross, but He did not refer to a wooden cross outside of ourselves, but to a cross within us in our souls. Gravelle was asked by a priest in what manner he was to die. He replied: "That I will die, I well know; but how it matters not, for I well know that God will stand by me in every pang." Because he so nobly bore testimony for Christ, his enemies urged that his tongue be cut out. He, therefore, quickly offered it to the executioner, so willing was he to suffer for his Lord. "I pray you, pray for me," were his last words.

Then came Phillipine's turn. As she was asked to offer her tongue to be cut off, she offered it joyfully. She said: "I care not if my body suffer, why should I care for my tongue." At the Place Maubert they were all burned at the stake. The two men were burned alive. Phillipine, after they had burned her face and feet with torches, was strangled, and then her body was burned, too.

"The blood of the martrys is the seed of the Church." Not without fruit was the death of Phillipine. Just as Stephen's death prepared for Paul's conversion, so the brave testimony of these martyrs spread Protestantism. For in the following year the French, or Gallic Confession of Faith was drawn up, and this was publicly recognized by the French court in 1561. O, if our Reformed forefathers and foremothers could suffer so much for our faith, how we should love our faith; and like them, be willing to deny ourselves, in order that it might be spread abroad to save the world for Christ!

V.

CHARLOTTE D'BOURBON, PRINCESS OF ORANGE.

CHARLOTTE was the daughter of the Prince Louis, Duke of Bourbon; but her mother, Jacqueline, was a believer in the Reformed doctrines, and she secretly taught them to her children. Charlotte's father, finding this out, determined to thwart his wife's influence by sending three of his daughters to convents. For the duke had met with such reverses of fortune that he would have found it hard to provide suitable marriage dowers for his five daughters, so he thought the best way to avoid their marriage, and also to keep them Romanists, was to send them to convents. Besides, at that time it was considered quite honorable for ladies of high rank to enter convents, and they lost nothing in social rank by it. The duke was highly commended by his Romanist friends for his self-denying act in giving so many of his children to the Church.

But man proposes and God disposes. It could little be expected that a nun would become a Reformed princess, but so it happened in her case. Her mother was heart-broken over this act of her husband, and she wept and prayed much, especially for

Charlotte, who was then only thirteen years old. Charlotte instinctively shrank from the life set before her, and begged to be allowed to stay with her mother. Her mother shrewdly prepared a solemn protest against entering the convent, which Charlotte secretly signed, and then Charlotte was compelled to go to the nunnery of Jouarre in Normandy. All her mother could do now was to pray. But the prayer of the righteous man availeth much, and the prayer of a righteous woman often avails more than that of a righteous man; so her prayers were answered, although she did not live to see the answer. For she died August, 1561, and Charlotte's release did not take place till ten years later. Meanwhile Charlotte in the nunnery made the best of her lot. Still she did not forget the last instructions of her mother, from whom she had been so cruelly torn. And when her mother died, and the papists would not even allow her to go and look at her mother's dead face, her dissatisfaction increased. Now, while she was quietly spending her time in the nunnery, a terrible struggle was taking place in France between the Huguenots and the Romanists. Although she was away from it, yet she watched it with great interest; for, although a nun, she sympathized with the Huguenots. But so secret was her sympathy for them, that she was supposed to be a good Catholic. And having influence as a princess of the royal line of the Bourbons, her friends succeeded in gaining for her the high position of abbess. This gave her the opportunity of teaching, but in a very guarded way, the new doctrine of the reformation, and many of the nuns imbibed her views. At length she came under suspicion, and was charged with perverting the nuns under her. She found herself in the greatest danger. The Romanists were about to begin proceedings against her. But just then (1572) providentially Normandy was invaded by the Huguenots, and her convent was thrown open by them. She saw the opportunity that providence gave her, and at once quitted convent life forever. To justify herself, she published the fact that she had been forced into the nunnery against her will, and revealed the protest she had signed many years before. This lessened the attacks of the Romanists on her, while it at the same time gained for her the confidence of the Huguenots, who saw that she had not been acting with duplicity. She at once fled to her oldest sister, the Duchess of Bouillon, who was warmly attached to the Reformed faith. She then fled from France, because of her danger, and went to Heidelberg, where she was welcomed by Elector Frederick III. of the Palatinate as a daughter. For Frederick, who had ordered the composition of our Heidelberg Catechism, was a great protector of the Reformed, and threw open his territory to them as an asylum.

When her father heard of her flight from the convent, he was beside himself with rage. As it was not known where she was, the French court took up her case and ordered that a search be made for her, and that she should be severely punished. Then it was that the Elector Frederick, a truer father to her than her own father, wrote to her father, March 15, 1572, notifying him that his daughter had found an asylum with him, and that he had received her, because she had followed the dictates of her conscience. Her father was now angrier with her than ever. He was indignant that she had left the convent. Had she remained a Catholic, he might have forgiven her. But that she should have become a Protestant, the very thing he had tried for so many years to prevent, was too much for him to bear. He even went so far in his anger as to impugn Frederick's motives by writing to him, "Can it be honorable for you to receive into your house children who have run away from their father? Is it not more worthy for you to advise them to return?" But Elector Frederick did not flinch in his devotion to Protestantism and answered her father in a dignified way, stating his willingness to return Charlotte, provided she would be granted free exercise of her Reformed religion in France. He also wrote in the same strain to the king of France. The king declared that he was willing to let her worship according to her Reformed faith, and even appointed messengers to go to Heidelberg to bring her to France, but her father was inflexible against her. "If she means to persist in the Protestant religion," he said, "I would rather she would remain in Germany, than return to France to scandalize everybody, and be the misfortune of my old age." The king's messengers came to Heidelberg, but she declined to go to France, as her father would not consent to her religion. So she remained at Heidelberg with the Palatinate court.

Three pleasant years she spent there under the kindly care of the Elector Frederick. Then Prince William of Orange sued for her hand in marriage. It was a very suitable match, for he was the ruler of the Netherlands, and she was a princess of the royal line of France. But there were grave difficulties in the way, for when does the course of true love run smooth? It was necessary, for the sake of political peace, to get the king of France and her father to give their consent before the marriage could take place. The king, in his answer, refused to commit himself either way, and the Dutch court went on the principle that silence gives consent, especially as he said he would raise no objections. The French parliament finally gave their consent. But would her father give his consent? However, although he had been most irreconcilable before, he now saw in it a brilliant marriage for his daughter to the leading statesman of Europe, and not only gave his consent, but gave her an ample dowry. Other difficulties arose, but the marriage nevertheless took place, June 12, 1575. It was a very happy marriage, for both were members of the Reformed Church and interested in the same aims, charities and hopes. She proved herself, as William's brother, Count John of Nassau, said, "A wife distinguished by her virtue, piety and intelligence."

But new cares and anxieties came to her with this marriage. For her husband was engaged in a deadly war with Spain. That country had done everything to defeat him and threw odium on his marriage, because he had separated from his former wife, who had been unfaithful. William, therefore, was compelled to defend himself and his marriage, which he did by showing the king of Spain to be one of the blackest souls that ever ruled a nation. This reply William scattered all over Europe. In June, 1580, the king of Spain finally, finding that he could not conquer William by fair means, determined to employ foul, and he offered a large reward of 25,000 crowns to any one who would bring him, alive or dead, to the king. Charlotte was greatly alarmed by all this. She was in constant fear for the life of her husband. Again and again did she warn him to be careful, and not let strangers approach him. But he had become so careless of himself during the previous wars that he would not heed her warnings. The next year what she feared happened. Two Spainiards, one of them a master of a bank at Antwerp and the other his servant, plotted to take William's life. The master was to share the reward, but the servant was to do the deed. Before the servant Jaurequay went to perform the fatal act on Sunday, March 18, 1582, he was absolved from all his sins by a Romish priest, who gave him the sacrament and also a charm to protect his life. The priest, fearing that his courage might fail him before he struck the fatal blow, accompanied him to the castle and gave him blessing on his diabolical work when they separated. Prince William had been to the Reformed church that morning, and was at dinner when the assassin tried to enter the dining room, but was repulsed by the prince's servants. But after dinner William was showing Count Laval some tapestry, which had on it pictures of the Spanish cruelties. Then Jaurequay again tried to force his way, but the servants prevented him. William, however, innocently and unsuspectingly reproved the servants, and ordered him to be allowed to come, as he thought the man was some citizen who wanted to see him. The assassin, seeing his opportunity, stepped forward, and, putting his pistol over Count Laval's shoulder, fired. The prince was wounded in the head, the bullet knocking out several teeth, passing through the lower part of the head, and out into the right cheek. It just grazed the juglar vein, passing so close to it as to cauterize it. For a moment William did not seem to realize what had happened, but it seemed to him as if the house had fallen. But immediately the prince, recovering himself, begged that the assassin be spared. However, the man was dead already. Charlotte, when she heard the report of the gun, rushed to her husband, and, seeing him covered with blood, fainted. When she recovered, she nursed him with the greatest care. It was found, however, that he was in no great danger, as the wound rapidly healed. The Reformed people of Holland were deeply grateful to providence for sparing their prince and leader. On May 2 they held a solemn thanksgiving service at Antwerp for his recovery, at which both William and Charlotte were present.

But the excitement and care proved too much for her. Almost immediately after that thanksgiving service she collapsed. She became sick with pleurisy and died in a few days. She was buried in that beautiful cathedral of Notre Dame at Antwerp. The cathedral, in which she was buried, contains many magnificent masterpieces of paintings, as Rubens' "Descent From the Cross" and his "Elevation of the Cross," but none of these masterpieces come up to her beauty of character, for her life was a living picture of sacrifice for, and consecration to, Christ. The spire of that cathedral is wondrously beautiful, being of marble, yet so delicately carved that its drapery makes it look, says one writer, as if the Brussels lace (for which Antwerp was so famous) had been turned into marble and laid on it as a tracery of white. Her character, like it, pure as marble and delicate with all the graces of spirituality, soars heavenward like that spire, and remains a loving witness to the power of the Reformed faith. She became the ancestress of kings, her daughter marrying the son of the Elector Frederick III. of the Palatinate, who had so kindly shielded and befriended her, and Queen Victoria of England is thus a direct descendant of hers. Thus a nun became a Reformed, and a princess became the mother of kings, but she is now a saint in the court of the King of kings.

VI.

LOUISA DE COLIGNY, PRINCESS OF ORANGE.

AMONG the children of Admiral Coligny of France was Louisa. Her father gave her a fine education, but he and her mother (whose motto was, "As for me and my house, I will serve the Lord") gave her what was better, the Reformed faith. During her girlhood her father was engaged in the Huguenot wars, fighting and suffering for the Reformed faith, yet his letters to her were exceedingly beautiful and sublimely Christian. Among his officers was one who, although young, possessed so much wisdom that he was admitted to the councils of the Huguenots, Charles De Teligny. He soon became a suitor for Louisa's hand, and won it. Her father gave her this advice: "You have other suitors, rich and titled, but I advise you to choose Teligny as your husband." They were married at Rochelle in 1571. Then came a season of peace after the wars, but it did not last long. For when Henry of Navarre was to wed Margaret of France, Coligny went to Paris to attend the wedding, attended by Teligny and Louisa. Teligny was warned against going there by anonymous letters, but, like Coligny, was, alas! too confident. At midnight, August 24, 1572, the church bell opposite the Louvre rang out the signal for the awful massacre, and 25,000 Huguenots in Paris alone were killed or wounded. Among the victims of this awful massacre were both Louisa's father and husband. Her father was brutally killed in his room. Her husband managed to escape out on the roof with Coligny's minister. Teligny was so popular that one of the guards, sent to kill him, had not the heart to do it. But the Duke of Anjou's soldiers then came up and put him to death.

In some way or other Louisa managed to escape, how it is not known, but she must have escaped alone and on foot. She made her way as rapidly as possible to her father's castle in Chatillon in Burgundy, so as to warn her step-mother and brothers to flee. It seems that her escape was so rapid that she arrived there before the news of the massacre. The sad news she brought was like a thunderbolt to them. But they had no time to mourn, only to flee, and hardly time for that. They deemed it safest to scatter in the flight. Her two oldest brothers at once fled and succeeded in escaping safely, as did her step-mother. Louisa, with her cousin, fled to Gen-

Louisa De Coligny, Princess of Orange. 115

eva. But her youngest brother, a boy of uncommon promise and the pet of his father, was in some way captured and taken back to Paris. Thus Louisa, at the early age of nineteen, was an orphan, a widow, an exile and in poverty, for her father's property was all confiscated.

She remained at Geneva and Bern for a while, but finally found her way to that asylum for the Huguenots at Heidelberg, where she was most cordially received by Elector Frederick III. of the Palatinate. The French offered her her property if she renounced her Reformed faith, but like Moses, she preferred poverty to all the riches of France. At Heidelberg she met Charlotte De Bourbon, who was also an exile and had found a refuge at Heidelberg. They were one in suffering and sympathy. Some time after, the Duke of Anjou, who was the leader of the band that put her father and her husband to death, passed through Heidelberg on his way to take the throne of Poland. Elector Frederick was conducting him through the picture gallery of kings, queens and princes in the castle, when the Elector pointed to Coligny's portrait and asked the Duke if he knew whose it was. "Yes," he replied, "the Admiral." Frederick could no longer control himself, but said, "It is he, the best of men, the wisest and greatest captain of Europe, whose children I have under my protection, lest the dogs of France should tear them to pieces, as they have done their father." The Duke became very much confused under these words, as well he might be. But the Elector continued, "Of all the lords of France whom I have known, that is the one I have found most zealous for the glory of the French name, and I am not afraid to affirm that the King and all France have suffered in him a loss that can never be repaired." The Duke tried to apologize for the assassination of Coligny by suggesting that the Huguenots were forming a conspiracy at the time. But the Elector cut him short by saying, "We know all about that, sir."

When Charlotte De Bourbon, the wife of the Prince of Orange, died, that Prince in 1583 proposed marriage with Louisa. She had been a widow for eleven years, and besides was poor. But that Prince was glad to accept her without a marriage dower, as she was the daughter of Coligny. So they were married at Antwerp, April 12, 1583, and immediately afterward took up their residence at Delft. The people of Holland, although inclined at first to look on the marriage with France with suspicion, soon learned to love her. Her personal charms and her polished manners made for her hosts of friends. Motley says, "She was a small, well-formed woman, with delicate features, exquisite complexion and very beautiful dark eyes, which seemed in after years to be dim with unshed tears, with remarkable powers of mind and angelic sweetness of disposition." Miss Benger says, "She possessed more firmness of character and mental vigor than Charlotte De Bourbon." The Dutch people had reverenced Charlotte, and they now loved Louisa. On February 28, 1584, she had a son born to her, Prince Frederick Henry, who afterwards became illustrious as the Prince of Orange and the leader of the Netherlands. The rejoicing of the Dutch was very great at the birth of this boy, for the Prince's children, with one exception, had been girls, so that if anything had happened to the older son, Prince Maurice, there would have been great danger to the state. But the birth of Louisa's son averted this.

But Louisa had her troubles and fears, as well as her joys. She was afraid her husband would be assassinated. This had been attempted in 1582, and had failed. The reward that the King of Spain had offered for his life, was still offered. Her fears proved only too true. For the man who was to perform the deed, was already in the palace. He was a Frenchman, though of a part of France which was under Spanish control. In the hope of the rich reward, and out of love for his Romish faith, he had meditated on the deed for six years. He came to Delft, May, 1584, and so ingratiated himself into the Prince's service that he became one of his confidential servants. But Louisa's suspicions became aroused, for woman's eye can see sharper through character than man's, and she asked her husband, "Who is that sinister-looking man, and what does he want?" "He wants a passport, and I will give it to him," the Prince replied. Soon after the Prince left the dining hall and met Gerard in the hallway, at the foot of the stairs. Gerard held the passport in his hand, as though waiting for the Prince to sign it, but his other hand held a pistol. The moment William turned his eyes away from him, he sent three bullets crashing through his body. The Prince staggered under the mortal wounds and cried out in French, "O my God, have mercy on my soul and upon this poor people." One of the Prince's ushers caught him in his arms and set him on the stairs. Louisa and William's sister, the Countess of Schwarzenburg, were at his side immediately. His sister, thinking him dying, asked him if he commended his soul to Christ. He answered, "Yes." That was his last word, for he died as his attendants then laid him on the bed. The assassination occurred July 10, 1584.

Poor Louisa was overcome with grief. At the early age of thirty-two she was twice widowed. The tragic death of this husband recalled to her most painfully the death of her former husband and her father by assassination. She lived over again the terrible massacre of St. Bartholomew. It was a terrible ordeal, yet she trusted God and bore her sorrow with a beautiful resignation. "She had," said Maurier, "the advantage to be sprung from the greatest man in Europe, and to have had two husbands of very eminent virtues, the last of whom left behind him an immortal reputation. But she likewise had the misfortune to lose them all three by hasty and violent deaths, her life having been nothing but a continuous series of afflictions, able to make any sink under them. But a soul like hers had resigned itself entirely to the will of God." Thus William was assassinated a little over two years after the first attempt at assassination, and Louisa was made a widow after being married only a year and three months, being left with a babe only four and a half months old. She was left poor and without the necessities of life. "I hardly know," she wrote to her husband's brother, Count John of Nassau, "how the children and I are to maintain ourselves according to the honor of the house." The Dutch provinces, however, kindly granted her a yearly allowance of $4,000. Thus she was lifted from her previous penniless condition and given a competence throughout life. She had many cares, for the education of the six daughters of William's previous wife, the oldest of whom was only eight years old, was committed to her. This duty she faithfully fulfilled, so that it was said she so stamped her own character on them that they resembled her more than their own mother.

Meanwhile great political changes had taken place in France. King Henry of Navarre had become King of France, and the Reformed had the right of existence according to the edict of Nantes. So Louisa was privileged to be able to go back to her native land in 1549. On a Sunday of that year, she happened to meet the Duchess of Montpensier, who at the massacre of St. Bartholomew had distributed badges among the Catholics for exterminating the Huguenots. When she came into the room, Louisa left it abruptly, because she could not stay in the presence of such a woman.

But Louisa's path was not all clear joy. The religious controversies broke out in the Netherlands between the Calvinists and the Arminians. Her own pastor became involved in them. For when she removed to The Hague, the capital of Holland, in 1591, she had founded a French Reformed church there and had as her pastor the celebrated Utenbogard. He was one of the leaders of the Arminian party, and so Louisa's sympathies were with them in the controversy; at least she desired religious toleration. When the Dutch government ordered all the Arminians or Remonstrants to leave the land, she interceded for them, especially for Barneveld, in the interests of peace and of religious freedom. The result was that she became unpopular among the Dutch people and no longer felt at home among them. So after a stay in Holland of thirty-seven years, she decided to leave Holland and go to her native land of France. And so unpopular had she become on account of the religious controversy, that when she left, the populace hissed her on the streets as she rode away. But her son, Frederick Henry, whom she left behind her in Holland, afterwards became the ruler of Holland, and reintroduced religious freedom and allowed the Arminians to come back. So she ultimately gained the victory for her principles of freedom. But before this took place, she had passed to her reward. She lived only a short time after she went back to France. At Fontainbleau she became sick. When it was known that she was sick unto death, the Catholics tried their best to win her back to their faith. Cardinal Richelieu, the most crafty of them all, was sent to do this. When he entered her chamber, he found on the one side of it the Reformed pastor of Fontainbleau, Courcelles, and on the other side a devout Protestant lady. Richelieu said, "Madam, take care of your soul. You have two evil spirits beside you." And then he professed deep anxiety for her soul and urged her to save it by returning to the Romish Church. But the wily cardinal, who knew so well how to mould history, found more than his match at the bedside of this Reformed princess. She declared herself unshaken in the principles of the Reformed faith, and in her hope of heaven and salvation through Christ's merits, and she therefore now asked to be spared such intrusions as his, which brought her neither security nor peace. Richelieu departed defeated, and the Reformed pastor, Courcelles, comforted her till she died, rejoicing in hope, October 9, 1620. Her body was embalmed and taken to Delft, where it was laid in a magnificent tomb with her husband. Through her son, Frederick Henry, she became the ancestress of Electress Louisa Henrietta of Brandenburg and of King William of England. "There never was," says Brandt, "one of a more noble soul or a truer lover of justice than this princess."

Chapter IV.—Italy.
I.
DUCHESS RENEE OF ESTE.

EVEN into Italy, the land of the Pope, the Reformation also spread. One of its protectors there was the Duchess Renee of Este. She was not Italian by birth, but French, having been born at Blois, October 15, 1510. Her parents had earnestly prayed for a son that he might be heir to the French throne, which excluded females from becoming heirs. When, therefore, a girl was born, they were greatly disappointed and looked upon her as an innocent intruder,—a sort of female Ichabod, showing that the glory had departed from her father's house. She was, therefore, slighted, and some have described her as ugly, and even as a hunchback, which, however, is probably not true. But for all that she was beautiful in character. "Beauty is that beauty does." And she was of some value, for she was a king's daughter and her hand therefore, was eagerly sought for. She came nearly marrying the young prince, who later became Emperor Charles V. of Germany. Then came the Duke of Bouillon, the richest man in France, and also Cardinal Woolsey, who asked her hand for King Henry

VIII. of England, to succeed Catharine of Arragon.

Renee had grown up a double orphan, her mother dying when she was only three years old, and her father when she was five. Still she was well trained, under the care of Queen Margaret of Navarre, and by Madame Soubise, her governess. Her studies were like those of Margaret of Navarre, and one of her companions was Margaret of Angouleme, who became devoted to the Reformed, as was Madame Soubise. Under such influences she early inclined to the new religion, as the Reformed was then called.

The summer of 1528, when she was 18 years of age, saw her married to Hercules, Duke of Este, whose home was at Ferrara, in northern Italy. Her mother-in-law was the famous, or rather infamous, Lucretia Borgia, noted for her brilliant talents and awful wickedness. It was a political marriage, but Renee went to Italy to be a faithful wife. Her husband's court was a literary centre and he invited many men of letters to Ferrara, and published their works. The court artist was Titian, and the elder Tasso was her secretary. Ariosto and Rabelais made the court brilliant by their genius and wit. Renee brought to this court the most brilliant gifts of mind, together with elegance of manners so common to the French. She inherited all the virtues of her father, joined to the goodness of her mother. Although in Italy, she still remained true to her Reformed religion, and for it she was harshly treated by her husband. As early as 1528 there had been a Reformed minister at Ferrara, but we do not know whether it was through her influence or not. As her father-in-law, Duke Alphonse was a devoted Catholic, she could surround herself with Reformed influences only in indirect ways. She selected as tutors of her children several persons who were Reformed. Her husband's chief physician, Manzolli, was Reformed. His works, which satirized the vicious life of the clergy, were forbidden by the Pope and his body afterward disinterred and burned for heresy. Some of the professors at the university at Ferrara were Reformed. Clement Marot, the hymn-writer of the Reformed, and Charles D'Espeville, whose real name was John Calvin, graced her court for a time. Calvin lectured on religious subjects, it is said, in the chapel of the palace, made beautiful by Titian's pictures; and the number of Reformed increased from day to day.

For a number of years, she had been permitted large liberty in her religious efforts, but now the suspicion of the Romish clergy was aroused. A king's daughter had liberty which a peasant's child had not, but the time came when the terrible inquisition began to move. Calvin, after a stay of a few months, was compelled to leave. Her husband permitted the arrest of Calvin while he was the guest of Renee. She, however, arranged for an assault on the men who were taking him to Bologna for trial, and he escaped over the Alps. Ochino, too, the general of the Capuchin order, who could "make stones weep," as the Emperor Charles V. said, was condemned to death for heresy, but she enabled him to escape to Geneva. Her husband permitted the inquisition to fill his prisons with prisoners, but he could not prevent his wife from visiting them in their distress. At last, all the Reformed were driven away. She greatly mourned, in a letter to Margaret of Navarre, her utter isolation in Italy. Still, by correspondence she was able to keep in touch with her Reformed friends. Her correspondence with Calvin was considerable. The Pope visited her in 1543 and gave her a costly diamond and jewels, but it did not bribe her to Romanism. The inquisition, however, surrounded her with spies and gradually the little Reformed congregation at Ferrara dwindled, until in 1550 the light of the Reformed faith was extinguished there.

Having destroyed her friends, the papists now turned to destroy her. About 1552 a Jesuit was forced on her as chaplain, but the Jesuit found Renee a better debater than himself, and reported that she was obstinately fixed in her opinions. Being unsuccessful in converting her to Rome, he demanded of the Duke that he exclude her from all society. So in 1555 she was carried by night to the castle and placed in solitary confinement. No books or visitors were allowed her, and her younger children were placed in a convent. She was allowed to converse only with the Jesuits. Threatened, abandoned by all near to her, the prey to fears, she weakened and received the mass and the Jesuits boasted of her conversion to Rome. Calvin all the while kept in touch with her by correspondence, trying to guide her mind aright, and to strengthen her under the persecutions. In 1559 her husband died, bequeathing her a fortune as long as she remained a Catholic. But Renee's faith was not dead, although her sufferings for it were enough to have destroyed many another's faith. She again spoke out boldly for her Reformed religion. Her son, forced by the Pope, gave her the alternative of becoming a Catholic or of leaving Italy. She unhesitatingly chose the latter. And amid great mourning on the part of the people of Ferrara she left Italy.

But when she returned to France, how changed France had become during her absence of thirty years. Her early companions were almost all gone. She determined, therefore, to make the Huguenots her friends, and throw over them the shield of her protection. She interceded for them with her arch-enemy, Catharine De Medici, corresponded with Elizabeth, queen of England, pleading for them, and encouraged Jeanne D'Albret. Renee's earnestness for the Reformed made it unsafe for her to stay in Paris, so she retired to her ancestral castle at Montargis, which she made an asylum for the persecuted Huguenots, so that they called it "Hotel Dieu" or the "Hotel of the Lord." She sheltered hundreds in it, and it is said that three hundred at one time sat down to her table.

The people of the town of Montargis were bigoted Catholics, and in their hatred of things Reformed they raised a riot against the castle, but were defeated by soldiers sent by the Duke of Conde from Orleans. Finally the Duke of Guise, her son-in-law,

RENE OF ESTE DEFYING MALICORNE

but the leader of the Catholic party, determined to destroy that "nest of heretics" at Montargis, and ordered her to leave the castle, as the king required that fort. He sent Malicorne, who threatened that if she would not deliver up the castle, he would batter it to pieces and put her Reformed ministers to death. Her royal blood boiled at this. "This decrepit, prematurely-old woman," says a writer, "cowed the general with six companies of soldiers at his back." "Malicorne," she said, "consider well what you do, for no man in the kingdom has a right to command me but the king, and if you advance I will put myself foremost in the breach, and see whether you will have the audacity to kill a king's daughter, whose death heaven and earth would avenge on you and your seed, even to the children of the cradle." Malicorne retired after such bravery on her part. Doubtless she would have been driven out of her castle, but fortunately for her, soon after the Duke of Guise was assassinated. Her great interest in the Reformed Church is shown by the fact that she appeared at the consistory meetings and took part in the proceedings. Calvin wrote to her, remonstrating with her for this, and kindly reminded her that Paul forbids women to exercise ecclesiastical authority (I Cor. 14:34-35 and I Tim. 2:11-14). She replied that the Queen of Navarre, and Admiral Coligny's wife, and the mother-in-law of the Prince of Conde had done the same thing, but that she would not do so again. In her activity with the consistory she but foretold by her action the present activity of women in the Church. When Calvin died she greatly mourned his death. So great was his regard for her that he wrote to her from his dying bed. She ever cherished his memory with great veneration. She lived to see the awful massacre of St. Bartholomew in 1572. Some writers think that she was in Paris at the time, but it is not likely, or she would have doubtless been killed. Her greatest sorrow was, that her daughter, the Duchess of Guise, who, since the assassination of her husband, had all the tiger nature of her grandmother, Lucretia Borgia, rise up within her, was one of the foremost in bringing about the slaughter of the Huguenots. No doubt Renee, with her usual kindness, protected and saved many of the Huguenots in that massacre.

She died at Montargis, greatly mourned by the Huguenots, June 12, 1575, aged about 65. Her tomb is there, with the arms of Ferrara and her cipher surmounted by a crown. But she has received a greater crown, even a heavenly, with the benediction of her Lord, who could say of her life and kindnesses "Well done." On one side of the inscription are the lilies of France, and on the other the ermine, its spotless white the symbol of the purity of her character, a symbol, too, of the robe she now wears, "washed and made white in the blood of the Lamb."

II.
OLYMPIA MORATA.

ONE of the most beautiful characters of the Reformation was Olympia Morata, the scholar and the Christian. Her name was classic, Olympia, but her spirit revealed all the old classic genius of Greece, baptized by the sweetness of Christianity. She was by birth an Italian, one of the fruits of that Italian reformation, which, alas! was crushed in its bud by the inquisition. Her father was tutor of the two sons of the Count of Este in northern Italy, and she was born at Ferrara, 1526. Her father, Morato, early trained her in the classic languages, which were then rousing such a furor in Europe. She made such progress in them, that within a few months she was able to speak Latin and Greek easily. When she became twelve years of age, her fame as a classic scholar was already noised abroad. At the early age of fourteen she composed a defense of Cicero in answer to his calumniators. She was considered a miracle—the most learned woman in Europe. She became so polished and learned that when Duchess Renee of Este sought a companion for her daughter in her studies, she chose Olympia. Thus Olympia's lot was cast in most pleasant circumstances—a female genius living with princes. She soon became the idol of the court that was filled with scholars. She delivered lectures at Ferrara on the classic authors in the private academy of the Duchess.

While she was thus living in the palace, the doctrines of the Reformation began to show themselves in Ferrara. Two Germans, named Sinapius, who taught Greek and medicine there, had brought them from Germany. The coming of Calvin and his brief stay there strengthened the evangelical influences. But it was the conversion of her father to Protestantism that most influenced her. From being a humanist, he became a Protestant. For while she was in the court, he had been banished from Ferrara, and settled at Vercelli. There he happened to receive under his roof a Protestant missionary named Celio, who had been an old acquaintance. Celio returned his kindness by leading him to something higher than the classics (which had been his idol),—to Christ. The conversion of Morato was followed by the conversion of others of his household. Meanwhile Olympia, at the court of the Duke of Este, was still idolizing the classics. She says of herself: "I had no taste for divine things. The reading of the

Old and New Testaments inspired me only with repugnance." But in the midst of her joys and honors, lo! her father was taken sick in 1548. She at once left the court and went to nurse him. He calmly waited for death, bearing a beautiful testimony for Christ. This death of her father was the beginning of her life of many sorrows. Soon after his death, her companion, the princess to whom she had been a companion, Anne of Este, was married, and she had now no friend at court to defend her against the suspicion of being a Protestant. She was compelled to leave the court, and although the favorite of its social circle, she went to care for her invalid mother, three sisters, and a brother yet a child. Thus she sacrificed honor and position for the gospel, choosing, like Moses, rather to suffer with the people of God than to enjoy the pleasures of sin for a season.

Among the strangers who had come to the university of Ferrara to study was a German, named Andrew Grunthler. Through Sinapius he had heard of Olympia. He learned to admire, then to love her. He sued for her hand, and was accepted and they were married in 1549. The prayers of the little Reformed church of Ferrara went up for this young couple, that God's blessing might rest upon them.

She wrote a hymn on the occasion, which reads like an ode of Pindar, only it had a Christian instead of a pagan theme running through it. It reads thus: "O Almighty God, King of kings, Creator of man and woman, Thou who gavest to the first man a companion that the race of mortals might not perish; Thou who hast willed that the soul brought out from humanity should be the mystic bride of Thine own Son, and that that divine Son should give His life for her, oh, shed peace and blessing upon these two now united before Thee. Thy law is the nuptial couch and the hymen of eternal love."

But the dangers were gathering around the little Reformed church of Ferrara. The Pope would not allow a Protestant church in Italy. Grunthler, therefore, prepared to leave and return to Germany, to seek a place in some university. He left behind him his wife, as he feared that the journey over the Alps in the cold winter would be too severe for her. He returned several months afterward, and then took her with him away from Ferrara. They started in June, (1550), accompanied by her brother, Emilio, aged eight years. They traveled through the Tyrol, passing the imperial army, and finally arrived safely at Augsburg. There the Fugger brothers were the rich merchants, who led the trade and art of the city. They had heard of Olympia's fame. They gave her a splendid welcome, and she and her husband had a charming sojourn there. They then went to Wurzburg, where her brother had an accident, in which he was saved from death by a seeming miracle. While playing with his companion, he fell suddenly from an elevated gallery headlong on the rocks below. They thought him killed, but, strange to say, he was not at all injured. She said she saw in it how God gives His angels charge over those who are His saints. Then, with her husband, she went (1551) to Schweinfurth, whose senate called him as physician to the Spanish soldiers. So Olympia, the great classic scholar, was compelled to let her talents blush unseen in a poor country village. Her stay, however, was made pleasant by the education of her brother and by the kindness of the Protestants of the town, especially the pastor. Here she translated into Greek many of the Psalms and attended to the education of her brother.

But, alas! the place that they expected to be the refuge for them, proved to be the place of greatest danger. The tide of war swept to this town. Margrave Albert of Brandenburg happened to choose

Schweinfurth as the place in which to defend himself against the Emperor. The neighboring princes of the empire combined to destroy him. Thus the inhabitants of the town were compelled to suffer most terribly for a quarrel to which they were strangers. The siege began April, 1553, and lasted fourteen months. It was a terrible experience. The walls and houses were continually battered by the enemy's artillery. The citizens feared to go outside of their dwellings, yet met death sometimes in their houses. Bands of the enemy would at times overrun the town, and forcing themselves into the houses, would compel the owners to give them their money. These scenes became more terrible every day. Famine added its horrors to war, and pestilence followed famine, until it cut off one-half of the population. In the midst of all these horrors her courage did not forsake her. She wrote: "Under the weight of so many evils we have found consolation only in prayer and meditation upon the holy Word." Her husband caught the fever, and, alas! all his medicines with which to allay it were exhausted. It seemed as if nothing short of a miracle could save him. Olympia went to One who was better than medicine—the hearer and answerer of prayer.

Olympia Morata. 141

Her prayers were answered, and, lo! her husband was saved. This gave her courage. The Lord, who had cared for, and spared, her husband, would certainly care for them in the siege.

But the terrors of the war became worse and worse. The enemy outside were angered by the bravery of the defenders. A rain of fire seemed to descend on the town at night. The houses afforded no safety for the inmates. They were compelled to seek refuge in the bowels of the earth. Olympia, with her husband and brother, spent several weeks in the depth of an obscure cave, afraid to go out. Finally the Margrave, seeing defeat before him, suddenly evacuated the town in the middle of the night. The enemy came in, but the citizens found that they brought no relief, only worse oppressions. For they pillaged the town and set it on fire. Fearful were the scenes in the town. The people pressed to the gates to escape, only to be driven back and condemned to perish. Some made their own funeral preparations in their homes. Some fell on their knees, trying to soften the hard, cruel hearts of the enemy, but in vain. Others ran toward the church as the asylum of safety, only to perish in the building, as it fell in the conflagration. Olympia and her family were drawn into the crowd that was surging toward the church, where they would have perished, when a soldier bade them flee or they would be buried under the ashes of the town. They followed this mysterious guide sent from heaven to save them, and he led them by a circuitous route beyond the walls. As they looked back, they saw the flames mounting up to heaven and the houses crackling under the heat. They hurried on and began to think themselves safe, when they were attacked by a band of soldiers, plundered of all they had, and her husband was taken away a prisoner. In her great distress she cried unto the Lord, "Help me, help me, for the love of Thy name." Exceedingly sad was her condition when she escaped from this danger. She had lost her shoes, her hair was dishevelled, and her clothes in tatters, with hardly a garment to cover her. During that awful night she traveled more than ten miles. She arrived at the village of Hamelburg, comparing herself to the "queen of beggars," for she entered it with a borrowed dress, pale, emaciated and sick with the fever. The citizens of Hamelburg did not dare keep them long, for fear of the enemy. So, although she was so ill that she was hardly able to walk, she was compelled to leave. As they followed the banks of the river, the gravel and stones cut her bare feet, until she cried out in agony, "I can go no farther. I am dying. Lord, if Thou wilt, save me; command Thine angels to bear me on their wings." At the next town she came to, the lieutenant had been ordered to put all the refugees to death. But as the bishop happened to be absent, he gave them a little respite, till he returned, meanwhile keeping them in suspense between life and death. He finally let them go.

Then the favor of heaven began again to shine on them. An unknown nobleman, touched with their sufferings, gave them fifteen gulden of gold. With it they were able to work their way to Erbach in the Palatinate, whose count was so pious that a minister in the neighboring town declared that he learned more in a few days than in six years at Wittenberg University. When at last she found a safe asylum, Olympia broke down completely. She was crushed. At one blow she had lost her husband's fortune, and also the books, which had been brought at great expense from Italy, all of which fell a prey to the flames at Schweinfurth. The fever which had been in her, now burst forth at its height. She was, however, very tenderly cared for by one of the noble families of the Palatinate, the Count of Erbach. The Countess gave to her the care of a sister, and when she again became convalescent, she was greatly pleased to find that her brother was now opening his heart to the Reformed faith. She found a religious atmosphere in that noble family, as the Count had family worship in his home, and daily visited his people, exhorting them to piety. The Count used his influence to have her husband, who had arrived there safely, too, appointed as a professor at Heidelberg. He succeeded in having him appointed by the Elector of the Palatinate, and they left Erbach for Heidelberg.

On the way a pleasant little incident occurred. One evening they came to an inn, where the schoolmaster and his pupils had come to give a concert. His pupils did not do very well—in fact, broke down. Olympia at once rose with her charming grace, and went to them, encouraging them and helping them. The schoolmaster was greatly surprised that she should know the pieces of the children. He talked with the visitors long afterward. And when he found out that it was Professor Grunthler and his famous wife Olympia, he ran to his house to bring some pieces set to music by Grunthler, which he often sang in his family. He was greatly pleased to meet their author.

Two days later they arrived at Heidelberg, August, 1554, and found there a very agreeable home, as Heidelberg was not only beautiful for situation, but it had become a great seat of learning. There, too, they found old friends in Sinapius, her former teacher of Greek, and Curione, who gave them a cordial welcome. She and her husband were, however, very poor indeed, and had to borrow twenty florins of gold to meet the expenses of the first month. While her husband lectured on medicine, she was compelled to attend to household duties. Leodius has spread a report that Olympia was called to Heidelberg as professor and became a female lecturer there. There is no question but she would have graced such a position with her genius. But she makes no reference to lecturing in any of her letters, neither do the acts of the university speak of any connection of her with the university. Her name is only once mentioned in its acts, and then her poems are referred to.

She kept up a large correspondence. The destruction of the little Reformed church of Ferrara by the Pope caused her great sorrow. Some of its members were put into chains, some sent into exile, and others found safety in flight. The temporary apostasy of her dear friend, Duchess Renee, caused her pain. Her companion, Anna of Este, had become the head of the house of Guise in France, who so terribly persecuted the Reformed there. She wrote thus to Anna, pleading for them: "Since the Lord has honored you with so great a blessing as knowledge of the truth, you cannot be ignorant of the innocence of these men who are every day dragged to the scaffold, and who are exposed to cruel torments for the cause of Christ. It is your duty to intercede for them. If you remain silent, and allow them to suffer and die without defence, you are becoming the accomplice of their persecutors. I know that in pleading their cause you may provoke the anger of the king and the fury of your enemies. I answer, it is better to be exposed to the hatred of men than that of God. "If God is for us, who can be against us?" The result of her plea was, that for years after, the only one in the French court who dared to lift up her voice against the persecutions was Anna of Este.

Olympia was also busy with the education of her brother Emilio. She taught him the classics. But it was especially the Bible that she delighted to open to him. That was her consolation in those days of poverty and weakness. She had, however, little time for the study of literature, as her time was taken up with household duties. She was, however, not permitted to live long in this delightful home. Her sufferings during the siege at Schweinfurth and her flight had so weakened her that she did not seem able to rally. The danger increased when the plague broke out in June, 1555, at Heidelberg. By July she had become so weak that her life was despaired of. She felt that she would not get well. Writing to Curione, she says: "As for me, I grow weaker day by day. The fever never leaves me for an hour."

Her death was radiant with hope. It was a mount of transfiguration. She felt not the pangs of death, but its joy and bliss. To her the Lord had taken away the sting from death and left only the honey. She saw heaven before she got there. A few hours before her death she awoke from a sleep and smiled most beautifully. When asked the cause of so sweet a smile, she said, "I, in a dream, saw a place illumined by the purest, most beautiful, brilliant light." Her husband answered, "Courage, my well beloved; you will soon dwell in the midst of that pure light." She smiled and nodded assent. Soon after her sight failed. "I can see no longer," she said to her husband, **"but all that surrounds me seems decked with beauti-**

ful flowers." These were her last words. She immediately fell into a sleep and passed away. She died October 25, 1555, at the early age of 29 years. But though she died so young, she had gained the fame, and passed through the sorrows, of a long lifetime. Great was the sorrow of Protestants everywhere—in France, Switzerland and Germany—at her death. The plague continued its terrible ravages. Her husband, dazed with grief at the loss of his wife, now went everywhere, recklessly exposing himself as a physician to the awful plague. He did not care to live, since she did not. He seemed to be courting death. And death came to him within a month after her death. Emilio also fell a victim. All three of this interesting family are buried in the historic St. Peter's church at Heidelberg, where to-day the traveler can read this inscription: "In the name of the eternal God and to the memory of Olympia Fulvia Morata, the beloved wife of Andreas Grunthler. Her remarkable attainments in several languages, the marvelous purity of her life and her piety elevate her above her sex. The witness of her life was even surpassed by that of her death. Peaceful, happy and holy she died in the year of our Lord MDLV., aged xxix. years, in a strange land. Here she lies with her husband and her brother Emilio."

PART II
Women of the Seventeenth Century
CHAPTER I.—GERMANY.
I.
ELECTRESS ELIZABETH OF THE PALATINATE.

NOT so well known as the famous Queen Bess of England, but far more beautiful was her namesake and relative, Princess Elizabeth, the daughter of King James I. of England, yet her lot became as sad as she was beautiful. The sad fate of her family, the Stuarts, seemed to hang over her. She became the unfortunate Queen of Bohemia, the "paschal lamb" of the Thirty Years' War.

She was born August 19, 1596, at the palace at Falkland, Scotland. Her early life was made happy by an idolized brother, Henry, who instilled into her young mind an antipathy to Rome, which was only intensified as she afterwards suffered so much from Romish powers. She was sent to school at Combe Abbey. When there she was hurried away when the gunpowder plot (1605) was discovered, because the conspirators hoped to capture her and force her to become queen. When the danger was over, she wrote to her brother a little note which concluded with this expression: "If God be for us, who can be against us?" At that time a lad of nine years sent her from the continent a note of congratulation on her safety. He was the little Count Frederick of the Palatinate, who afterwards became her husband. He declared in this note that he believed that that wicked conspiracy proceeded from the direct agency of Anti-Christ. Later she wrote to her guardian a poem in which she seems to have caught the devotional spirit of Lady Jane Grey. When she was sixteen years old, Frederick sued for her hand. It was deemed wise to unite two such prominent and Reformed powers as England and the Palatinate in marriage. So on October 16, 1612, Prince Frederick embarked for England to receive his bride. The Protestants in England were very glad for the marriage of their beautiful princess to Frederick; although the Catholics opposed it, and Elizabeth's mother never lost an opportunity to remind her that she was marrying beneath her station by calling the Palatinate Prince Frederick "Goody Palsgrave." Elizabeth promptly replied, "I would rather espouse a Protestant count than a Catholic emperor." It happened that just as Frederick arrived in England, Prince Henry, the heir to the throne and the idol of the people, died. So most fortunately Frederick came to England to take her brother's place with Elizabeth. And the nation seemed to transfer its interest from the dead prince to Frederick.

They were married on Valentine's Day, 1613, with great pomp. Dressed in a gorgeous robe of white and silver, studded with diamonds, a crown of gold on her head, her long hair woven with pearls and diamonds, her train carried by thirteen young ladies dressed in white, she was married to the prince. The Archbishop of Canterbury married them, and a sermon was preached by the Bishop of Bath and Wells on the wedding at Cana. After the wedding Frederick visited Cambridge and Oxford, where he was received with great honor, and then prepared to take his bride back to his own land. Their journey through Holland and up the Rhine seemed a triumphal entry. Reception followed reception. At Amsterdam from her barge to the carriage she passed over a bridge richly carpeted, while on the front of the exchange was a beautiful arch, on which she was represented as Thetis, the goddess mother of Achilles. Every day there were military displays, so that her bridal journey seemed a victorious march. At Dusseldorf her husband had provided a yacht on which she was to sail up the beautiful Rhine to Heidelberg. When she arrived at the Palatinate, she was received by the towns of Oppenheim and Frankenthal with great rejoicing and honor. She arrived at Heidelberg on a beautiful day in June. Almost all the Protestant nobility of Germany was there to welcome her; and as they came with large retinues of followers, Heidelberg was full of gaiety and splendor. The Princess arrived before the city, having 374 in her company, among them English nobles, as the Earl of Arundel and Lord Lenox. As she proceeded to the castle in a carriage with eight horses, the streets were strewn with green-sward and the roofs crowned with boughs of May. Along the walls were hung festoons of flowers. The next day the court preacher, Scultetus, preached a sermon, and for twelve days the festivities continued. They were closed June 18, 1613, by a sermon by Scultetus on the subject of thanksgiving, based on the 119th Psalm. Nearly 300,000 pounds were spent, and 5,500 persons dined every day at the castle.

And now began her happiest days. Her "honeymoon" lasted five years. This beautiful castle, which provoked the wonder of the English visitors, had been enlarged by the English building and the thick tower at the west end, built by Frederick for his English bride. He also laid out the rough wild mountain back of the castle into a most beautiful garden—a blooming paradise where she might rest and enjoy herself. Here in summer, oranges and limes spread their fragrance. Here was an English orchard, there a mulberry grove. Beautiful beds of many tinted flowers varied the view. From the edge of the precipices fell an artificial waterfall, while silvery streams of water would flow when bidden through the garden, and as they flowed, musical symphonies, supposed to be breathed by naiads, fell on her ears. There were grottoes from which issued streams of melody. The beauties of the garden were so great that King Louis XIV. of France became jealous lest it would eclipse the splendor of his gardens at Versailles. Here passed the happiest years of her life. Her happiness seemed to culminate when in 1619 she became a queen, for her husband was elected king of Bohemia. Her mother could no longer sneer at her for marrying only a prince, for she was now a queen. She gained the coveted rank, but alas, heavy hangs the head that wears a crown. But she was ready for it, for she writes to her husband, when he accepted the throne, "I shall not repine, whatever consequences may ensue, not even though I should be forced to part with my last jewel."

The time had now come when Queen Elizabeth was to set out for Prague, to ascend the throne of Bohemia. Her departure from Heidelberg was ominous of her future sorrows. The day before she left was Sunday. She attended service on that day, and her chaplain, by a curious coincidence, preached on the text: "Go to now, ye that say to-day or to-morrow we will go into such a city and buy and sell, and get gain, whereas ye know not what shall be on the morrow," etc. Strange to say, "the year" in that text was fulfilled, for she remained just a year as queen in Bohemia before unexpected disasters came upon her. When she arrived at the Bohemian border with her husband, she was received with great honor. Her journey reminded her of her triumphal bridal journey up the Rhine a few years before. Her beauty and rank seemed to dazzle the Bohemians. At Waldsach the women and children gathered around her, touching the hem of her garment, or prostrating themselves before her as if she were some new divinity. Her journey was completed and crowned by a magnificent triumphal procession into Prague, October 21, 1620. "Never," says her biographer, "since the days of St. Elizabeth has any princess inspired sentiments of such impassioned affection in the people of Prague. The horses of her carriage were adorned with housings of gold and silver, and she sat under a canopy of gold and silver not more splendid than becoming to her fair complexion." Her husband was crowned November 3, and three days later she was also crowned in great state. Amid music she approached the chancel of the Hussite church, and knelt to receive the crown of Bohemia. The Administrator of Bohemia, who crowned her, preached a long sermon, which he closed with the wish that "the piety of the new queen might be rewarded with the longevity of Sarah, that in all her undertakings she might be prosperous as the beautiful Rebecca, that she should prevail over her enemies like the intrepid Judith, and be meek and magnanimous like Queen Esther, and that finally she might be persevering like the Queen of Sheba in the search of truth and wisdom, and above all, be crowned with spiritual gifts like the blessed Salome, who had been chosen and solemnly approved by the Savior of the world." He then solemnly crowned her as the walls resounded with the shouts, "Long live Queen Elizabeth."

But, like her husband, she soon found that heavy lies the head that wears a crown. She found it difficult to retain the adoration of the Bohemians. Her ignorance of the Bohemian language separated her from them as if by a Chinese wall. The customs of her court were so different from theirs. They were simple, rude country people, while her court had the levity of French manners. So social customs soon clashed. As an illustration of this, the story is told that soon after her arrival, the wives of some of the citizens of Prague presented her with a testimonial which consisted of some specimens of their baking, as cakes and bread. These they brought crammed rudely together in a bag. The queen returned to them her thanks, but alas! her courtiers treated the kind givers with scant courtesy. A page mocked at the gift by seizing one of the loaves of bread and twisting it into fantastic shapes, and putting it on his head like a wreath. The rest followed his example, and the poor Bohemians went away with their feelings hurt. Her religious views also alienated some of them. Like the Reformed, she disliked crosses and crucifixes. Now the Bohemians had a great crucifix on the bridge over the Moldau, which they looked up to as a patron saint. She was charged with avoiding that bridge, so as not to pass the crucifix.

These troubles were but the preparation for darker days to follow. Her husband was called away to the army, which was to protect Prague. He soon saw the dangers that hovered over them, and wrote to her that if she felt afraid, she should leave Prague, but she nobly refused to leave him behind. Though heartsick and anxious, she had to preserve the mask of outward joy and pleasantry to her court and the people. Finally her husband's army was defeated on Sunday, November 8, 1621, just outside of the city of Prague. She was attending church service, when the battle began, and the minister had just read, "Render unto Caesar the things that are Caesar's," etc., when the thunder of the cannon shook the church, and the minister left the pulpit and with the congregation rushed to the city walls to view the battle. Frederick hastily put her in a carriage and sent her to the citadel for safety. And now began her woes, that like wave upon wave went over her. The next morning at nine o'clock he brought her carriage, that she might escape. As she entered it, never again to return to Prague, one of her admirers, young Count Thurm, offered to defend the citadel for a few days, in order that she might make good her escape. But she nobly forbade this, saying, "Never shall the son of our best friend hazard his life to spare my fears. Rather let me perish than be remembered as a curse to this city."

Over terrible roads Elizabeth and her husband fled to Breslau. Sometimes the road became impassable and she had to get out and ride on horseback in the cold, wintry weather. A terrible snow-storm came up. Finally they arrived safely at Breslau, but the reception by the inhabitants was as chilly as the weather. It was evident she could not stay there, but where should she go for safety? She wrote to her father, King James of England, begging him for help, saying that if he forsook her, they would all be ruined; but he would not help her, although the Puritans of England were strongly in favor of aiding her. Where could she go? She finally found a brief resting place at the fort of Custrin, where the Elector of Brandenburg, her brother-in-law, allowed her to stay, but refused her any money. There she bore a son. She then, forgotten by her father and cast out by her brother-in-law, traveled westward toward Holland. How different her journey now from her bridal trip a few years before. Then all was gladness, now all is sadness. The Dutch government, however, received her as a queen, and kindly allowed her a pension. Here at last she and her husband found an asylum during the awful years of the Thirty Years' War.

Here one trial after another seemed to come upon her. The Dutch populace called her and her husband "royal beggars." In 1628 she lost her oldest son, a brilliant boy, the heir to the throne, who went with his father to Haarlem to see the Dutch fleet return after its capture of the silver fleet of the Spaniards. The young man was drowned before his father's eyes, crying out, "Father, save me." There came a ray of joy to her when Gustavus Adolphus gained his victories. But this was taken away by the absence of her husband, who went to meet Gustavus. And the next year Gustavus, who had been a sort of guardian angel, was killed. A few days after, came the news of her husband's death. Her previous calamities were trivial compared with this. She showed, as a writer says, "marvellous grief." Yet she confessed in a letter to the Dutch States that "her first great resource was heaven." Spanheim, her biographer, says: "Her letters are admirable for the strength of judgment, and for their dignified resignation and touching piety."

She seemed to be left alone, without husband or country, with none but her children. And these gave her increasing anxiety. One son was defeated and another captured by the emperor. Then came the death of Duke Bernard of Weimar, who had been a guardian to her after her husband's death. Then came the bitter woe of a son and a daughter going over to Romanism. Her brother, King Charles I. of England, was beheaded. And yet her life was not entirely hopeless. She found at the Hague the society of cultured people. The Reformed ministers showed her much kindness. She lived quietly for many years at a country villa at Rheten. Here she pursued her favorite sport of the chase. Here she educated her children. Her house was called "the mansion of the muses and graces," because of her fair daughters. For there the great philosopher Descartes taught her daughter Elizabeth. But alas! her troubles were not yet past. The close of the Thirty Years' War gave back the Palatinate to her family, but only added to her discomforts. For as her son, the Elector Charles Lewis, did not care for her as he should, she suffered with increasing want.

At length, bereaved of every object that endeared Holland to her, she accepted an invitation in 1661 to return to England. How different her return from her departure many years before. No shouts go up from assembled crowds, nor does any homage come from the nobles. She who had once been a power in the negotiations of nations and a queen of beauty in society, was forgotten. After living a short time quietly, she died February 13, 1662. "She was a princess of talents and virtues not often equalled, rarely surpassed." Her beauty and her tact made her a power in history. Brave men, as Gustavus Adolphus and Lord Craven, like the knights of the middle ages, were led by her beauty to take up her cause. Thus Duke Christian of Brunswick snatched a glove from her hand, kissed it, stuck it into his hat as a plume, and then drawing his sword, took a solemn oath never to lay down arms till she was again on the throne of Bohemia. He placed as his motto on his flag: "For God and for her."

II.
ELECTRESS LOUISA JULIANA OF THE PALATINATE.

SOME women are statesmen, if we may be permitted to use that expression instead of stateswomen. Louisa Juliana was one of them. She inherited it from her father, who was one of the greatest statesmen the world ever produced, William, Prince of Orange. She was the oldest daughter of his second wife, Charlotte De Bourbon, being born at Dort in Holland, in 1576. She had a loving mother till she was six years old. Young as she was, she was deeply sensible of her mother's death and grieved greatly. At the time of the assassination of her father she was about eight years old. Young as she was, she wrote a letter to her uncle, Count John of Nassau, saying, "We have suffered so great a loss, my sister and I, that we know not to whom to confide our grief, unless to you, whom we supplicate most humbly to be to us all a father and a kind uncle, in order that we may be brought up in the faith in which our father had us educated." Evidently hers was an old head on young shoulders.

She was reared by her aunt, the Countess of

Schwarzenberg, and gained all the polish of a finished French education, so that she had the seriousness of the Dutch blended with the vivacity of the French. The fame of her accomplishments and attractions brought to her feet many suitors. Her accepted suitor was one of the leading princes of Germany, Elector Frederick IV. of the Palatinate. She was married to him at Dillenberg June 13, 1593, and went with him to his capital at Heidelberg, where she was received with great festivities. She introduced some of the polish of the French customs into the somewhat ruder Palatinate court. The nobility had been given to the rougher amusements, as hunting, fishing, hawking and sometimes to drunkenness. She tried to banish intemperate and profane habits from the court and to establish habits of sobriety and decorum. She also endeavored to produce a higher religious tone in the court by establishing the practice of the daily reading of the Scriptures. She was careful to imbue the minds of her children with religious impressions. Her horror of the papacy was very great. We have seen it in the little letter her son Frederick V. wrote as a boy to Elizabeth in England about the Gunpowder Plot, calling the Catholics Antichrist. The intensity of her Reformed convictions was so great that she instilled into her son's mind an aversion not only to Romanism but also to Lutheranism especially in its latitudinarianism about worship, which in her estimation were not far removed from the errors of Rome. She was careful for his polite training, by having him sent to the court of the Count of Bouillon at Sedan where he was kept from the rough drinking customs of the German nobles and learned the polished manners of the French. Her husband dying when her son was only fourteen years of age, his cousin, Duke John of Zweibrucken, acted as regent during the boy's minority. But she was his adviser, and by their united care the land prospered and gained in influence. She greatly rejoiced at the marriage of her son Frederick to the daughter of the English crown. When the Elector returned from England with his bride, his family at Heidelberg, in receiving him was headed by Louisa Juliana with a train of twelve princesses and noble ladies in the vestibule of the castle. But her mother-heart forgot the conventionalities of society and broke through all etiquette as she threw her arms around her daughter-in-law's neck as she burst into tears of joy.

Frederick now assumed the government of his land, and his mother retired to her little estate at Kaiserlautern. Here she took a warm interest in the people under her care and they improved in piety, refinement of manners, and general prosperity. Here she lived in seclusion and peace until the outbreak of the Thirty Years' War. When her son, Frederick V., was offered the throne of Bohemia, she, with her natural sagacity in political affairs, strongly urged him against accepting it. She foresaw all the later calamities that came to the land—loss of his land of the Palatinate, and the persecutions of the Reformed. In eloquent words she pictured to him his lack of allies and the danger if he accepted. Well would it have been for him if he had heeded his mother's advice. But no, against her will, urged on by his wife, he accepted the Bohemian crown. When he left Heidelberg for Prague Juliana uttered the fateful prophecy, "And now the Palatinate removes to Bohemia," and went to bed, sick with anxiety, after she had parted with him in tears and sighs.

When the Bohemian war terminated so disastrously against him a year later, she lost her little county of Kaiserlautern and fled to Heidelberg, from which she escaped with difficulty; but found a resting place with her daughter who had married the Elector of Brandenburg. She lived during the war, partly in Berlin, his capital, but most of the time at Königsberg, in far east of Polish Prussia, farthest removed from the dangers of the war. There she greatly aided in founding a Reformed congregation, for the whole land of Prussia was Lutheran. But she had Reformed service in her castle chapel, out of which grew a permanent Reformed congregation there. While she was there, her daughter-in-law Elizabeth, came fleeing from Bohemia and bore a son at Custrin, named Maurice. This boy the grandmother took to her home at Königsberg and reared. Says Miss Benger, the biographer of Elizabeth, "It is a trait of generosity that Juliana never became estranged from Elizabeth, however opposed they may have been in their opinions. There was in each of these princesses no common share of firmness and dignity, and of the younger might be personified Hope, the older was no less characterized by Resignation."

When Gustavus Adolphus came from the north to deliver Germany from the power of the Catholic armies, a very serious breach occurred that threatened to allow room for the destruction of the Protestants of Germany, by alienating them from Gustavus. He, at the very beginning of his campaign, came into collision with the Elector of Brandenburg because of the fortress of Spandau, which the Elector claimed and Gustavus refused to give up. Gustavus at once marched his victorious army against one who ought to have been his ally and threatened to bombard the gates of Berlin. The Elector then saw his danger and tried to gain peace, but in vain. Several embassies were sent to Gustavus, but he seemed determined to humiliate the Elector by attacking his capital. Then Gustavus was surprised to receive a delegation of ladies. How often the ladies can do what the gentlemen can not, especially when it comes to subjects requiring delicate tact. These ladies were the Electress Louisa Juliana and her daughter, the Electress of Brandenburg, who had repaired to his camp. By the wisdom and beauty of Juliana's address Gustavus was disarmed. He found in her a stateswoman greater than his own statesmanship. Yielding to her intercessions he gave up his hostile purpose, and became a friend to the Elector, and thus became united to the Protestants of Germany. She rejoiced at the

LOUISA JULIANA AND HER DAUGHTER INTERCEDING WITH GUSTAVUS ADOLPHUS

victories of Gustavus in Germany, but after his death had to mourn the death of her unfortunate son, Elector Frederick V.

She remained at Königsberg until her death on March 5, 1644. At her death she was greatly comforted by the consolations of the Reformed faith. She was greatly strengthened by the prayers of the Reformed ministers who visited her. To her daughter-in-law Elizabeth, who had suffered so much by the war, she sent a message, thus: "Assure her," she said, "that I have always loved and honored her from the heart, and that these affections I will carry with me to the grave. Inform her children that it was among the last prayers on my lips, that God would bless them, that it would greatly have delighted me to have seen them restored to their estates. But God having ordered it otherwise, I assure them that He will never forsake them." She ordered her court preacher, Agricola, to preach at her funeral on 1 Peter 1:18, saying, "My reason for this choice is that therein is contained all my consolation which rests only on the precious blood of Christ." So died one of the greatest princesses of the Reformed Church—a female William of Orange in her piety, ability and statesmanship, yet uniting with these virtues the quieter graces of the female sex.

LANDGRAVINE AMALIE OF HESSE

III.

LANDGRAVINE AMALIE ELIZABETH OF HESSE CASSEL.

ONE of the greatest leaders of the Thirty Years' War was this noble princess. Her biographer calls her the greatest noblewoman of her country. She was the granddaughter of Prince William of Orange, from whom she inherited "his wisdom and his eagle eye." She was born January 29, 1602, at Hanau in Germany, and was married at the age of eighteen to Landgrave William V. of Hesse Cassel. Her husband having espoused the side of the Swedes in the Thirty Years' War, was finally compelled by the Austrians to leave his land and seek an asylum in East Friesland. At this most unfortunate moment he died September 21, 1637. It looked now as if the Hesse Cassel would be lost entirely, and with her the rights of the Protestants and of the Reformed. For with the exception of Saxe-Weimar, hers was the only land in Germany still in rebellion against the emperor, the rest having accepted the peace of Prague (1635). But she refused to accept that peace, because her Reformed faith was not guaranteed in it. She was the last one in Germany fighting for the Reformed faith. If she were crushed, what would become of the Reformed Church? It was a terrible crisis for the Reformed. Once before, in 1566, the German emperor had tried to crush out the Heidelberg Catechism, but the eloquence of Elector Frederick III. of the Palatinate saved it. Now it remains for a woman to be the second savior of the Reformed of Germany. For man's extremity proved to be woman's opportunity. There arose a Reformed Joan of Arc to lead the Reformed back to victory. She did not do it, however, by appearing on the battle-field, as did Joan of Arc, but by the shrewdness of her diplomacy. She has also been compared to the warrior woman of the Old Testament, and called the Reformed Deborah.

Fearful were the odds against her. A large part of her land was in the hands of the enemy. She and her family were exiles, and a debt of 590,000 thalers was on her land. When her husband died, he left his son, a mere boy, as his successor. But the emperor declared that her husband's will was void, and ordered her greatest enemy, the Landgrave of Hesse Darmstadt, to take possession of her land and rule it. This usurpation thoroughly roused her. With the courage of a lioness she proceeded to battle for her son's rights. As regent she began the war again. Her husband had fortunately left to her 15,000 excellent experienced soldiers. She also had as her commander Melander, one of the greatest generals of the war, whom the emperor had tried by high bribes to draw from her service (for the emperor knew his value), but in vain. She made an armistice with the emperor, during which negotiations for peace were to take place. He was so anxious to make peace, that he asked the Elector of Mayence, who acted as mediator, to get her to name her conditions. She replied that she would not make peace until Hesse Cassel had gotten back all the territory illegally taken from her, and till the Reformed (who had been ignored by the peace of Prague, 1635) had been given their rights. She thus held the balance of power, and her favor was courted by the emperor on the one side and by the French and Swedes on the other. With wise statesmanship she knew how to utilize her unique position. The emperor wanted her to give up the French and Swedes as allies, but she feared lest if she did, he would punish her afterwards. So she finally made a treaty with the French and the Swedes, instead of the emperor, after the armistice had lasted two years, the French giving her 150,000 gulden as a subsidy.

She then moved forward her army, 42,000 strong, into Westphalia, supported on the one side by the French and on the other by the Swedes. It gained a number of victories over the emperor's forces, among others recapturing Marburg, February 23, 1646, and regaining Upper Hesse. Her position was now so strong and her influence so great, that when negotiations for the Westphalian peace began, she entered into them on an equality with the Swedes and French, although she was the ruler of only a small German state. One of the emperor's friends declared that it was a shame that such a small state should dictate to the empire. Victorious in war she gained even greater victories in the peace negotiations that closed the war. She compelled Hesse Darmstadt to give up the land it had taken from Cassel. The emperor granted her her Reformed religion, and more than that, granted its toleration in all Germany, too. For the first time in the history of Germany, the Reformed were mentioned by name in this peace of Westphalia as the equals of the Lutherans and the Catholics. This was due to her persistence in keeping up the war, although she was aided in the negotiations by the influence of the Elector of Brandenburg, who was the great protector of the Reformed. The Bavarian General Gronsfeld said of her: "Amalie has gained immortal fame. She has gained toleration for her Reformed religion, which had been cast out by the empire. She holds the balance of power in her hands."

At the close of the war she laid down the regency of her land and gave its rule to her son, Landgrave William VI. The excessive cares of the war had weakened her health. For in the midst of all her political duties she still watched over her family with the greatest care (she had been the mother of fourteen children). She was careful to have them trained in the Reformed faith, the superintendent of Cassel, Neuberger being the tutor of the son who succeeded her. She desired to spend the rest of her life in quietness. But her health continued failing. She went on a visit, 1651, to Heidelberg, to her daughter, who had married the Elector of the Palatinate. There she was greeted as the Deborah of the Reformed Church. But while there, her rheumatism, which showed itself in her foot, increased; so with her daughter and other nobles she received the communion from the Reformed court preacher Pilger, and declared herself satisfied to follow whither God would lead. With great presence of mind she prepared herself for the end. When the operation was performed, she bore it with great patience. She never took her eye off of the wound, and told her physician he should cut more, if necessary, as she was ready to bear all. She gradually grew a little better, and was able to return to Cassel, July 12, by being carried in a chair by soldiers. On August 3 she had them carry her to church, that she might once more join with God's people in the worship of the sanctuary. She afterwards became worse, but declared in the midst of her great sufferings that she was ready to die. Just before she died, she reached her hand to both of her court preachers and said, "Good night." Then she fell asleep, August 8, 1651. She greatly loved her Reformed Church, which was the constant recipient of her bounty, and for which she was willing to sacrifice her all. She died greatly idolized by her people. On her coins is the motto:

> "Against might and craft
> God is my rock."

IV.

COUNTESS URSULA OF HADAMER.

THE Reformed princesses of the Thirty Years' War are exceedingly interesting characters. Among them and occupying a front rank, is the subject of this article. The Romish Church has a beautiful legend of the Countess Ursula, who with 10,000 virgins made a pilgrimage to Rome, and on her return was attacked by the Huns. The bones of this princess and her followers are still shown in one of the churches of Cologne, and the Romish Church venerates her as one of her saints. The Reformed have also a St. Ursula, and can match the legend by a story of fact, which reveals an equally faithful saint, who would not give up her faith. Her territory was a small province in western Germany, the country of Nassau-Hadamer. Her husband was a brave noble, but fond of display, and especially fond of showing his keenness in debate. It happened that the Austrian government brought a charge against the Counts of Nassau for having aided King Frederick of Bohemia against Emperor Ferdinand of Germany. These Counts sent her husband to Vienna to defend their cause and also to intercede for their land, which the Emperor's forces were so severely ravaging. The Count left his wife behind to rule in his stead. This she could do very well, for she was a woman of rare ability, as well as of nobility of character.

While her husband was absent (he was away about a year), alarming reports came to his land that the Jesuits were trying to convert him to Romanism. For the Emperor had utilized the Count's visit to Vienna to bring him in contact with his confessor, Lenormain. The Emperor honored him with an invitation to dine with him, and placed the confessor opposite the Count at the table. Of course very soon a debate sprung up between them, in which the Count prided himself in showing off his ability. But he was no match for the wily confessor. The Romanists so influenced him that he finally, after seven days of consideration, joined the Romish Church. After this had happened, he did not tell it to his wife. But one of his attendants wrote a letter to his pastor, acquainting him with the facts. The pastor called together the Reformed pastors of the country, and made known to them the contents of the letter. All were astounded. In that day it was the law of Germany, "like prince, like people." If a prince went over to the Romish faith, he could force that faith on his subjects. Of course, therefore, the Reformed ministers were justly alarmed at the prospect of the introduction of the Romish faith into their land. They discussed the situation, but felt that the Count's wife should be notified of his conversion, because she could protect them, and besides "was such an example of piety and a zealous promotor of the honor of God." But no one was willing to undertake to impart the sad news to her, partly for fear of the Count, and partly for fear of the results on her, as she was not very well.

Finally, Niesener, the pastor of Rennerod, offered to go. He went to her and broke the news as delicately and gradually as possible. But when he announced to her, that her husband was a convert to Romanism, she fainted away. When she came to consciousness again and was able to talk, he urged her, not to follow the example of her husband. She at once spoke out the noble determination, "I would rather be divorced from my husband and go out of this land a beggar, than leave my faith." She also thanked Niesener especially for his faithfulness in coming to tell her the truth, and promised to protect him, and if he were driven out of the country, to find a place for him in her brother's land of Lippe. Her husband, before he left Vienna to return home, wrote to her, telling her that he was now a Romanist. He finally returned in December, 1629, bringing with him two Jesuit priests to introduce Romanism. He placed his land under the ecclesiastical control of the Elector of Treves, who was to aid him. With bitter tears his wife received him, but all her entreaties failed to gain him back to her Reformed faith. He soon gathered the ministers together and announced to them his change of religion, and urged them to follow him. None of them had the courage to reply, except Niesener, who declared that they would follow God rather than man, and said, "I remember the words of Christ in Matthew 6:25, 'If the light that is in thee be darkness, how great is that darkness.'" The Count replied, that if they would not become Romanists, they must all leave the land within four weeks. He also invited the ministers to his table, one after the other, so as to bring them into a discussion with the Jesuits there, who might be able to drive them into a corner in argument or to convert them to Rome, if possible. The ministers unwillingly obeyed and came, but were generally silent, rather than make matters worse by an unfair discussion.

The Count also ordered the ministers to introduce the Gregorian calendar. This calendar, although introduced since in all Protestant lands, was at that time considered a sign of compromise with Rome. The ministers were, therefore, to observe Easter and Whitsunday according to it. But some of the Reformed refused to obey this, and this made confusion in the observance of Easter, because there was a difference of ten days between the old and new calendar. The Count dismissed the Reformed ministers, when he found they would not become Romanists. A cry of distress went up from the Reformed people, as they saw their pastors depart. The sufferings of these pastors was great. They were driven out in winter time, without a home or money or friends. One of them, the pastor at Salbach, wandered with his wife and four children for a year hither and thither, before finding a parish. On January 31, 1630, the Count gathered the people of the town of Hadamer together, and ordered them to follow him into the Catholic Church. He was followed by an address by the Jesuit Brack, who painted in rosy colors the beauties of Catholicism. On February 5 the Jesuits held their first service in the Reformed church at Hadamer. Everywhere the Jesuits took the Reformed churches and used them for Romish worship. The Count also commanded the inhabitants to attend Romish worship, under pain of imprisonment, yes, of death.

The result of all this was, that by the end of 1630 not a Reformed minister was to be found in the land with two exceptions. One of them, Artopeus, the blind chaplain of the Countess (he was now 88 years old), who was allowed to preach only in her room, but to hold no public Reformed service. But while the Romish priests seemed to have everything their own way, yet their lives were not safe. For the Hollanders with their soldiers would come suddenly into the land, and they would have to flee. To avoid this, they were ordered to dress in the clothes of private citizens and not to live at the parsonages, but in private houses. But the Dutch soldiers soon found out where they were. On one occasion they captured some of them and took them away as prisoners. When the Count remonstrated with the Dutch about this, the Dutch replied that they intended to keep them as hostages for some Reformed ministers who were kept in prison. Niesener was the only other

Reformed minister besides Artopeus who was permitted to remain in the land. And this was only because of the protection of the Countess. He was, however, banished to a village near the Catholic border, and forbidden to go out of his house. He and his family would have starved, had not some of the Reformed brought them food. One day he was warned to escape, because the Spanish soldiers would come and kidnap him and murder him that night. He, however, refused to leave, as he had given his word to the Count, and felt he ought not to break it. That night his house was surrounded, he was taken captive and hurried away. They did this because they said he was in league with the Dutch, and was a spy. They put him in chains and dragged him away, while his house was ransacked and his little ones driven out into the street. He was taken to Cologne, where he was imprisoned for a year before he was declared innocent. He was then set free and became pastor, as the Countess had promised, in the land of Lippe, at Horn.

Meanwhile the Countess, like her country, was suffering, bearing the woes of her Reformed people. Often she interceded for them, but in vain. Her own children, whom she loved with all the tenderness of a Christian mother, were taken away from her and taught to despise their mother's Protestant faith. Her chaplain was finally forbidden to hold services for her any more, although she greatly desired his services. Yet, though left alone, she was not alone, for she strengthened herself daily by reading the Bible and by communion with God in prayer. Finally, in 1638, she was laid on her dying bed. She greatly longed for a Reformed minister to comfort her in her dying hour, but none was permitted to come to her. On the other hand, her husband allowed the Jesuit priests to visit her. They began to argue with her against her faith, although she was weak unto death. They tried every method to get her to come over to Rome. But she nobly answered them out of her Bible and from her Heidelberg Catechism. The Jesuits finally withdrew and reported to the Count the obstinacy of his wife. But though they were unsuccessful, they yet bore testimony to the beauty of her Christian character. One of them said, "It is truly to be regretted that this silver should be tarnished even to its last life's breath by the filth of unbelief." And another bore testimony to her character by saying, "that such a heretic as she outweighed many a dozen of Catholics in God's sight." "Countess Ursula," said another, "reveals in everything the most perfect model of Christian piety. She gave herself diligently to prayer with her servants or alone for three hours daily, and on Sunday she spent almost the whole day in that way. In a word, she was a splendid example of all the virtues, a benefactor of the poor and widows and orphans." The poor were fed at her table, and even the plague did not keep her back from faithfully visiting the sick. She was an angel of mercy, going about doing good. Thus died one of the saints of the Reformed Church, bearing faithfully her trials, yet shining with brightest hope. She is described as of slender, tall form, and of uncommon beauty. From her black eyes beamed gentleness and kindness, joined to dignity and majesty. True goodness of spirit, strength of character and fullness of energy were hers. Thus she remained true and faithful to the end, and came off conqueror and more than conqueror through Him that loved her. The Reformed Church does not canonize her saints, but she should ever keep in grateful remembrance this saint of the 17th century.

V.
COUNTESS GERTRUDE OF BENTHEIM.

IN the northwestern corner of Germany, on the borders of Holland, lay the county of Bentheim. It was a thoroughly Reformed district, and ruled, in the latter part of the 17th century, by a Reformed prince, Count Ernest William. His wife was Gertrude, a lady of Holland, to whom he was married, August 22, 1661. The Count's brother, the Count of Steinfurt, became her bitter enemy because of her marriage, for he hoped that his brother, Ernest William, would die without heirs, and the county would fall to him. So he tried to discredit her marriage and prevent her children from becoming heirs, because she had not been of noble birth before her marriage. To protect herself she put herself under the protection of the neighboring Bishop of Munster, a strong Romish prince. She little thought that a Romish prince would always seek for some return for his trouble. The Bishop brought it about that the Emperor of Germany, on Jan. 22, 1666, granted her a diploma elevating her to the rank of nobility. Thus her marriage was recognized and her children would succeed to the throne of Bentheim. The Bishop, however, waited for some return for this act. He decided to try and proselyte the Count to Rome. The Count was of a weak nature, fit only to be a football in the hands of others. The Bishop succeeded in getting the Count to appoint a Catholic as his chancellor. This caused a sensation in Bentheim, and already the conversion of the Count was talked of. His wife saw the increasing influence of the Bishop with fear.

Finally the Bishop capped the climax by an act of violence. The Count's envious brother died and was buried at the beginning of August, 1668. The Count went to the funeral at Steinfurt, which was located only 18 miles from Munster, and stayed there five days. The Bishop saw his opportunity and secretly garrisoned the roads between Steinfurt and Bentheim, so as to capture the Count on his return home. And yet the Bishop did not pretend to take him by force, but simply to force on him an invitation to visit Munster, as he had often urged him to do so before. When the Count came to the place where the Bishop's forces were, the Bishop met him and urged him to take a seat in his episcopal carriage. The Count begged to be excused, as he said he ought to go home because he was in mourning for his brother and because of the baptism of a babe in his family. But the Bishop was inexorable. By gentle force he compelled the Count to go with him to Ahausen that day. On the following morning the ride was taken in company with the Jesuit Corler to Coesfeld and to Munster. The Count was separated from his attendants, and as his servants left him, they admonished him not to give up his Reformed faith, at which he simply folded his hands and gave a deep sigh. He was placed in a house next to the chapel in the castle. The work of proselyting him was pushed forward with great zeal. The Jesuit Corler tried hard to force him to Rome. The Bishop so stormed at him from dinner till evening, August 10, that the Count finally consented, and on the next day went over to the Romish faith. The Emperor, in recognition of this act, made him his councillor and chamberlain.

The news of his conversion soon came to Bentheim and caused great anxiety to all, but especially to the Countess, as she knew not what it would bring forth. Fearful of future exigencies, she, with great shrewdness, sent her four oldest sons to Holland, and placed them under the care of the States General of the Netherlands. The youngest, which was a newly-born babe, she quickly had baptized in the Reformed faith. She then very anxiously awaited results. The Reformed Church, too, felt the conversion of the Count keenly. A special meeting of the Classis of Bentheim was called. It resolved to make known to the neighboring Reformed bodies the apostasy of the Count and to pray the Synod of Cleve to get for them the protection of the Elector of Brandenburg. This appeal of the Classis was, on October 24, 1668, addressed to the court preacher of the Elector, John Hundius. The Classis also at this meeting chose for its seal a ship on which the Lord was with His disciples, surrounded by the storm. It had the inscription: "Lord, save us; we perish."

In the meanwhile the Count was kept away from Bentheim, and a party of Munster soldiers was sent to Bentheim, having the authority of the Count to gain possession of the castle there and garrison it. But the Countess, suspecting that her husband had been forced to this by the Bishop, refused to surrender the castle and declared, with just wrath, that she would not open to any one until she had talked with her husband face to face about it, and was really sure he wanted it opened. Then the Bishop came with an army of four thousand men to Bentheim to compel her to surrender. He brought the poor imprisoned Count with him, but kept him at his headquarters and compelled him to wage war against his own wife. All this must have made the Count's heart bleed, but what do Jesuits care for bleeding hearts, so long as they gain their ends. The Countess would have defended the castle to the death, but for the treachery of one of her men. The court master, Wolf, whether corrupted by the Jesuits or anxious for his life, gave the enemy the key. So the gates were opened. But even when the Munster troops rushed into the castle, the Countess rushed from her apartments to defend the castle gates. It was, however, too late. The castle had fallen and the Bishop came with her imprisoned husband into the castle court.

It was very evident on the next day that a change had taken place in the government. The day was a Sabbath, and the Bishop of Munster did not recognize the Westphalian Peace, which granted religious liberty. For when the Reformed court preacher went to preach in the castle chapel, he was prevented from doing so by the Jesuits, and the Jesuit, Corler, read mass there instead. The Bishop left fifty soldiers as a garrison in the castle. He hoped to have as little trouble in converting the Countess as he had had in proselyting her husband. But she proved a stronger fortress than Bentheim itself, for she could not be moved, as the Lord was her rock. They used all kinds of arguments and persuasions. Then they began to threaten her, but everything failed. After the Count had been with his wife a few days, they tried a new plan, namely, of separating her from her husband until she would become Catholic. So her husband was ordered to go to Munster, and leave his wife in the hands of the garrison at Bentheim. The most prominent Reformed officials of her land were dismissed. The condition of the Reformed ministers in Bentheim became worse and worse. Her court preacher, Sartorius, was transported by soldiers out of the land. Part of the Reformed Church endowments were given to the Jesuits. Pastor Spiekman, of Neuenhaus, was imprisoned, and Pastor Frank, at Schuttorf, was put out of his parsonage. The Upper Church Council was filled with Romish councillors, who now took charge of the church.

All this, however, was not enough. The Romanists felt they did not dare leave the Countess any longer at Bentheim. So this poor, much persecuted, but courageous woman was taken by armed men with burning torches from her chamber, after having been given hardly time to dress, and with her young babe, under military escort, was sent to Munster. She hoped that at Munster she would be able again to meet her husband, and in this hope she patiently bore the ride. When she arrived there, she was placed in the house of the mayor as a prisoner. The Bishop now gave her the command that she could not see her husband until she had caused her children, whom she had sent to Holland, to be brought back, for he wanted to gain control of them, so as to convert them to Rome. She, however, remained steadfast and refused. Then new trials were put upon her to force her to call her children to Munster. Most of her remaining servants were taken away from her, and then they threatened that if she would not order her children to come to Munster, they would take away from her her newborn babe; yes, they even went so far as to threaten to put her to death. But all these threats were in vain. In God's strength she bore them all. As persecution could not prevail on her, they now had recourse to another plan. The chancellor of the Bishop prepared a request to the States-General of

Holland, which said that the Countess had become reconciled to the Count and an agreement had been reached between them about the children, and that she asked that the Dutch government would send the children to Munster. This lie was placed before her to sign. She, however, cast it aside with noble scorn, and as she spoke of the wickedness of such methods, she received from the councillor the Jesuitic answer: "Right or wrong, it must be signed." The end justifies the means. The conversion of the children to Catholicism would cover all the previous sins of deception. They then forced her to sign, and a noble was sent to Holland with this letter to the Dutch government. But fortunately the States-General of the Netherlands knew how she was being treated and refused. Then the Jesuits tried to plot, so that the children might be kidnapped.

But while all this was going on at Munster, suddenly one day the Countess disappeared. As the family of the mayor, with whom she was staying, left Munster to go to a wedding, she seized the opportunity for flight. For after she had signed the paper, they had become a little more lenient with her imprisonment. After she had ordered her chamber-lady to be silent about her flight, and simply to say she was ill, one evening she clothed herself in the garment of a servant girl, and as the twilight was falling, she left Munster with her child and her nurse. At a distance from Munster she turned aside into an inn to stay over night. There she met a farmer from Bentheim, who had brought merchants' goods to Munster and was about returning. She asked him, without telling him who she was, to take her and her child and nurse and allow them to drive with him till morning. The farmer took her first to the village of Ohne, in Bentheim, and then over the border into Holland. There she revealed herself to him and gave him a written promise to pay him. Then she fled to Deventer, and finally to the Hague. The farmer who had aided her to escape was fined 500 gulden. Whether he paid this or got free from it by joining the Romish Church, is not clear, probably the latter. The flight of the Countess was not discovered till the third day. The chamber-lady of the Countess was arrested and watched by soldiers, but could give no information about the flight.

The States-General of Holland gave her protection. The Reformed states of Germany, Brandenburg and Hesse Cassel took up her case, but in vain.

For the Bishop of Munster, by a decree, June 8, 1678, pronounced the Count divorced from her, and hardly was this done than the Count was married to a Romish princess. She entered a protest against this decree for the sake of her children, and presented it to the Dutch government, and then went to bed sick, August 5, 1678. But the wrath of the Bishop followed her. For he had the Emperor issue a decree, April 17, 1678, depriving her and her children of all rights of nobility, and thus depriving them of succession to the throne of Bentheim. She was so completely broken down by the persecutions and the disappointments that she died the next March 29, 1679, committing her children to the care of States-General of the Netherlands. She was a martyr to the Reformed faith.

The Reformed in Bentheim were persecuted. Their consistory was deposed and Catholics put in their places. Many ministers had their salaries lessened. Others, because they had given advice to the Countess to send away her children, or because they corresponded with her, were banished or imprisoned. The whole county groaned under the quarterings, marches and levyings of the Bishop of Munster.

But such trickery as the Romanists used never prospers. God never blesses it, and Providence frustrated their plans. The Count, when he married Gertrude, had made a compact that only the male descendants should ascend the throne, and the females only when the males had died off. The child of the second marriage of the Count was a girl, so at the Count's death the land fell to his Romish cousin. There began a long controversy between the sons of Gertrude and the ruling princes of Bentheim, which lasted many years. This was not settled until in 1803, when, through the mediation of Prussia, England and Holland (as the Catholic line had died out), the throne reverted to the descendants of Gertrude, so that one of her descendants now rules the county of Bentheim. Thus closed one of the most pathetic stories in German Reformed history.

VI.

DUCHESS CATHARINE CHARLOTTE OF PALATINATE-NEUBURG.

SHE was a princess of one of the lesser Palatinate families, and was born at Zweibrucken (southwest of Heidelberg), January 11, 1615. She early showed herself a lover of God's Word. When sixteen years of age she was married to the Duke of Palatinate-Neuburg, who had gone over to Romanism and who showed all the intemperate zeal of a proselyte. Yet she remained true to her Reformed faith all her life, although she often suffered for it. She took with her to her new home at Dusseldorf, her Reformed chaplain, Hundius. He held service for her there three times a week in her private chapel, and every day he read and expounded a portion of the Word of God to her, so that in five years he had gone over the whole Bible with her. When the Reformed pastors of Zweibrucken suffered so greatly on account of the persecutions of the Thirty Years' War, she gathered together many things to aid them.

But her most remarkable act was her deliverance of Rev. John Lunenschloss, the pastor of the Reformed church at Soligen, near Dusseldorf. Her husband, as an ardent Catholic, tried in every way to oppress his Protestant subjects. But in spite of his oppressions, the brave Lunenschloss held his congregation together. In 1626 the Catholics broke into their church and held mass there, and finally crowded out Lunenschloss and his Reformed people altogether. When they could no longer worship in their church, they held service in the city hall. But even there the rage of the Romanists followed them, for they entered the hall and broke up the pulpit and the benches in it, until the leader, in his fury, broke his axe in his hand. But still, in spite of all this, the brave pastor still ministered to his flock. The Catholics failing in every other way, finally had Lunenschloss arrested and forbidden to preach. Still, he contrived to gather his congregation together at various places for worship. In 1629, the Dutch captured the town and restored to the Reformed their church. When they retired, the Catholics annoyed them by burning straw outside the church, and finally took it again. In 1644, the Reformed, as they could not hold services in the church, held them on the church steps. There, for half a year, they worshiped, Lunenschloss preaching sometimes in the cold, even in snow and rain. May the Lord give us like faithfulness to our Church and its services.

On June 11, 1645, the Reformed broke into the side door of the church, and held service. On the following Sunday, however, the councillors of the Duke of Palatinate-Neuburg, appeared and forbade them to hold services there. That night the soldiers came to the house of the faithful Lunenschloss, broke into it, and tore him away from his weeping family, while he tried to strengthen them with the first question of the Heidelberg Catechism, that "without the will of our Heavenly Father not one hair can fall from your head." The Lord honored such faith. The soldiers took him to the market-place of the town, with the intention of shooting him. But just as they were about to do it, orders came from Dusseldorf, that they should not shoot him, but bring him to Dusseldorf for trial.

As they traveled toward Dusseldorf and came to Hilden, a carriage passed them on the road. As it drove past, a noble lady looked out of the window and inquired what was the matter. When told that the soldiers were taking a Reformed minister to Dusseldorf for trial, lo! she stopped the procession, and ordered them to let the prisoner come with her into her carriage. She was none other than the Duchess Catharine Charlotte, who was traveling home to Dusseldorf. Very gladly did she receive this minister into her carriage, for it gave her an opportunity to converse with him about the things of God and about the Reformed faith so dear to them both. Behold now the interposition of God,—the minister, who a few hours before expected to be killed in the market place, and who had been dragged as a mere criminal along the road, now enters Dusseldorf, not as a prisoner, but as the companion of the princess. Thus God honors and protects his children, so that "not a hair falls."

When Lunenschloss was brought before the Duke he asked the minister why he had disobeyed his commands. He made the noble reply, "Your Highness, it is my duty to obey God. He has made me a watchman over my congregation and I must give an account to Him of every soul committed to my charge. Therefore, woe to me if I leave her through fear of man. On the contrary I am ready to sacrifice my life for the sake of my congregation and of my God." The Duke was surprised at his steadfastness and earnestness. He offered him gifts and honors, if he would renounce his Reformed faith and go over to Romanism, but Lunenschloss declared that nothing would ever make him give up his faith. The Duke, instead of punishing him, was so impressed by him that he offered to do some favor for him, if he had any to ask. Whereat, Lunenschloss modestly asked that his descendants might be admitted to the guild of stone-cutters at Solingen (for the Reformed were shut out from all such positions through the Romish regulations). The Duke granted his request and also permitted him to return to Solingen to minister to his people. He continued pastor there until 1651, when he died.

The Duchess, who befriended him was a beautiful character. Her kindness to the poor was well known. She dispensed favors to Reformed and Romanists alike. She had poor orphans taught trades at her own expense, and she visited the widows and dried their tears by her sympathy and prayers. The Romanists, with her husband, tried to proselyte her to Rome, but all in vain. She was too strongly grounded in the Reformed faith. Against them she drew up her own confession of her Reformed faith. And in that faith she died in 1651, having lived in the Catholic court for twenty years. Her pastor, Hundius, was very faithful to her and she highly valued his ministrations. When she came to die, he read to her the thirty-eighth Psalm, in which were the words, "Lord, leave me not." The Lord did not leave her, but strengthened her in her last hour, while her husband (who even in her dying moments fondly hoped to win her to Rome), prayed, "Lord, remember not her unbelief." She prayed, "My Lord, give me more grace than I am worthy of." She was one of the martyr-spirits, for all those years she suffered for her faith, yet she was found faithful when death came. Hundius preached her funeral sermon on John 3:16, and said, "that this princess had so loved the Lord and His Word, that it tempered all her trials." She loved it so much that she never missed a sermon, save when hindered by sickness. And when she saw any one in the church without a Bible and paying no attention to the exposition of the text, she was greatly dissatisfied. In her last moments, though surrounded by her husband and the Jesuits, she urged her servants to remain true to the Reformed faith. She was a great favorite in the land, and the Presbyterium of the Dusseldorf Reformed congregation paid a beautiful tribute to her memory. She, with the Countess Ursula of Hadamer, and Countess Gertrude of Bentheim, were beautiful sufferers for the Reformed faith from Romish husbands during the Thirty Years' War.

VII.
PRINCESS ELIZABETH OF THE PALATINATE.

THE most intellectual princess the Reformed Church ever possessed was Princess Elizabeth of the Palatinate. She was the brightest light of the Palatinate house after the days of Elector Frederick III., who ordered the composition of our catechism. She was a pupil of Descartes and the correspondent of Leibnitz, the celebrated philosophers, and on intimate terms with other learned men of her day. She combined with her native ability the broad principles of the house of Brandenburg (in which her abbey was located), namely of religious toleration; for her home became the asylum of all refugees. And yet to all her learning she added piety, which beautified and sanctified it. She was the disciple of both the philosophy of Descartes and of the religious faith of the Pietists.

She was the eldest daughter of Elector Frederick V. and Electress Elizabeth of the Palatinate, and was born December 26, 1618, at Heidelberg. Elizabeth suffered the sad fate of her father's family. When her father left Heidelberg to go to Bohemia to take the throne, she was left behind in the care of her grandmother, Electress Juliana. And when the coming of the Spaniards compelled her grandmother to leave the Palatinate and flee, she was taken along with her to Königsberg, where she found an asylum. She remained with Juliana till she was nearly ten years old. It was the sublime faith and religious earnestness of her grandmother that early helped to lay the foundations for the serious thoughtfulness of Elizabeth. Then she was sent to the Hague in Holland, where her father's family were living quietly in exile in the little village of Rheten. And yet her sad reverses continued. Her dearest brother, next older than herself, and her playmate, was drowned. Then came her father's death, and with that her hope of worldly position faded away. And her mother seems to have failed to recognize her ability for a long while, so that there was a coldness toward her.

But she bore all these things philosophically, and her adversities turned out to be blessings in disguise. For her family, when driven to Holland, had settled in one of the most learned lands of Europe. Holland was at that time the home of painters, poets and thinkers. She was the classic land of the Reformed theology of the seventeenth century. To this land of learning there came one of the greatest thinkers of modern times, Rene Descartes, who was ultimately to revolutionize men's methods of thought. Elizabeth had already made great progress in her studies before she met Descartes. She made no pretension to beauty, but had an expressive eye and a pleasing countenance. She had developed so quickly and brightly, that Ladislaus, the king of Poland, had sought her hand when she was only fifteen years of age. But the suit came to naught, because she refused to barter away her Reformed faith and go over to the Romanists.

After that she was wedded to philosophy, and gave up the thought of marriage. Descartes was introduced to Elizabeth and the Palatinate family by the Count Dohna, an adept in the Cartesian philosophy, and became her teacher. He was soon delighted and surprised to find in her a scholar so capable of exploring with him erudite questions and of comprehending sublime truths. This appointment of Descartes as her tutor proved very helpful to him. For in this noble family he first found the supporters necessary to help him on to fame. He, therefore, in order to be near them, lived at Eyndegeest, about a mile and a half from Rheten, for two years.

And when he went to North Holland afterwards, he continued his correspondence, especially with Elizabeth, and would often visit the Hague, so as to meet his favorite pupil. This little court of the Palatinate family, although in exile, thus became famous for its beauty and learning, so that it was called "the home of the muses and graces." Among them all, Elizabeth had the greatest talent for learning. Bromley says that "of the three illustrious sisters of that family, Louisa was the greatest artist, Sophia the most perfect lady in Europe, but Elizabeth was the most learned." She made such progress in philosophy, that she became famous as "the Star of the North." In order to appreciate the greatness of this, it is to be remembered that up to that time women had taken little part in learning. For it was supposed that it was above the sphere or power of woman to excel in philosophy. So her learning astonished the world. It happened, too, just at that time, that another woman appeared as a great thinker, Anna Schurman. And yet, although Schurman was talented with both the chisel and the pencil, Madame de Guebriant confessed that she was inferior to the Palatinate princess, Elizabeth. Elizabeth continued her correspondence with Descartes, and in their letters they discussed the deepest questions of philosophy and theology, such as the union of soul and body, God's omnipotence and omniscience, and man's free agency and virtue. Descartes dedicated his leading philosophical work, "The Principles of Philosophy," to her. She would often in her letters express doubts as to his positions and offer criticisms, while he on his part was not backward in reminding her when she seemed to him to be wrong in her ideas, yet the correspondence was mutually agreeable and helpful. Thus when in 1645 her younger brother went over to the Romish faith and she was by it thrown on a bed of sickness, Descartes criticised her for her want of liberality toward the Catholics.

In 1647 she left Holland for Brandenburg, where at the court of her uncle, the Elector of Brandenburg, she seems to have found quite a congenial home. She soon gained fame among scholars there, through a disputation that she had with the celebrated Thomas Kresbesch, which revealed her ability and gained for her great applause. She, too, succeeded in disseminating Descartes' books to some extent in eastern Germany, where as yet he was comparatively unknown. She thus perhaps scattered seed that harvested itself afterward in the new university of Duisburg, whose first professors were followers of Descartes. It was while she was staying there that she learned with great sorrow of the death of her teacher Descartes in 1650. True to him in her friendship, she, however, had never allowed his philosophy of doubt to undermine her faith, but she rather sought to utilize what was good in it to strengthen her faith in religion and in God. Had the rationalists of the next century used Descartes' principles thus, they would never have landed in the maelstrom of thought that threatened to shipwreck them.

After the Thirty Years' War was over, she went to the old family home at Heidelberg, which she had left when four years old. Here her philosophical tastes and literary talents brought her into intimacy with the professors of the university, especially with Professor John Henry Hottinger. He compared her to Olympia Morata, who had come to Heidelberg university in the preceding century, and who was a great scholar and correspondent of Melanchthon. Through a relative she was also made acquainted with the celebrated theologian, John Crocius, whose broader theological views suited her taste. But her stay at Heidelberg became uncomfortable for her, for her brother's parsimony made it unpleasant. And when her brother put away his wife, Princess Charlotte of Hesse Cassel, and married the Raugrafin Louisa of Degenfeld, she sympathized with Charlotte and aided her to escape; and so felt the disgrace of her brother, that she left Heidelberg (1662) and went to Cassel, where she lived with her sister-in-law. In 1667 she was very fortunate in receiving the appointment from the Elector of Brandenburg as abbess of Herford. This had been an old Romish abbey, which had become Lutheran in the Reformation.

During the Thirty Years' War the Elector had begun appointing Reformed princesses as abbesses, and so now appointed her. This appointment relieved her from being a pensioner on any of her relatives, and also gave her standing in the German empire. For it made her a political member of that empire. She was authorized to send a deputy to its diets, and required to furnish one horseman and six foot soldiers for the imperial army. She also had to preside over a court of justice, and exercised authority over about seven thousand inhabitants. Her territory was small and her income therefore limited, but she exercised great economy and banished all luxury from her little castle. Her chief diversion was knitting, and on Saturdays she sat as judge. Here her patience and justice were admirable, being tempered with mercy, and she often adding religious instruction. Here this cultivated princess lived, surrounded by rude, ignorant country-folk, and yet she enjoyed it, for she was able to relieve distress and better their condition. She gathered around herself in the castle a company of like-minded souls. The highly-gifted Anna Shurman eagerly accepted an invitation to visit Elizabeth, so like her in intellectual and religious tastes. Both had been disciples of Descartes, but Anna was the more enthusiastic and visionary; Elizabeth the more profound and fonder of abstractions. She also threw open her land to all who desired refuge. It was this liberal spirit that brought her providentially into contact with the pietism of Labadie and also led to her association with William Penn. Labadie and his congregation from Holland having left the State Church were looked down upon as separatists; for at that time the idea of a free Church, independent of the State, was not dreamt of, and many of the separatists had been fanatics. So when they came to settle in her land (1670), its inhabitants, the magistrates and the Lutheran ministers rose against their coming and appealed to her. As she did not grant their wishes, they appealed to the Elector of Brandenburg, asking that these strangers should be ordered out of the land. But the Elector at first permitted them to stay, as he saw Elizabeth wished by it to spread the Reformed faith, although he urged Elizabeth to be watchful over them. She graciously protected them against their enemies, and gave to the world an illustration of the beautiful principle of religious toleration. She was in turn affected by their earnestness and zeal, for it is evident, that as she became older, she was deepening in spirituality. She had to endure a good deal of ridicule for thus protecting the Labadists, even from some of her own noble relatives. Thus her sister, the beautiful Duchess Sophia of Hanover, visited her and tried to laugh at the religious earnestness of the followers of Labadie. But although she remained friendly to them, she was not able to give them an asylum for more than two years, for the other governments compelled her to send them away. But in it all she showed her love of religious liberty.

Her treatment of the followers of Labadie called

the attention of William Penn to her. He, too, was about to lay out a colony in the western world, called Pennsylvania, for which her little land of Herford set the example of religious liberty.

Penn's visit to her at Herford, 1677, is quite interesting. He stayed there three days. On the first day at 7 a. m. he called on the princess, and was surprised to be received with such warm expressions of welcome. He said the conduct of persons in such an exalted station confirmed his hopes that the day of the Lord was approaching. He therefore took courage and began preaching. And they had a religious service which lasted from 7 to 11 o'clock. In the afternoon Penn and his companion returned to her castle, and found the princess had invited her intimate friend, the Countess of Horn, and several others to the service. He held services there till 7 p. m., and all, both preachers and hearers, were deeply affected. The next day being the day when the princess received audiences and petitions, they did not get to see her till 9 a. m., but then all the inferior servants were also present. In the afternoon he fulfilled his promise made to her in the morning and narrated the story of his conversion to to the Quaker faith, together with the persecutions which he had suffered for it. His story was interrupted by supper. He then took supper with her, and afterwards again continued before them the story of his conversion. This lasted till 11 o'clock, p. m., when they returned to their lodgings. On the next day, the last of their stay, not only the residents of the castle, but also the inhabitants of the town, were present. The service began with much prayer. Penn says of this meeting: "Yea, the quickening power and life of Jesus wrought and reached them; and virtue from Him, in whom dwelleth the Godhead bodily, went forth and distilled upon us His heavenly life, sweeter than the pure frankincense, yea, than the sweet-smelling myrrh which cometh from a far country. And as it began, so it was carried on, and so it ended." After the meeting was over, the princess gave him good-bye, and was so overcome by her feelings that she could hardly give expression to her words. And as she bade him farewell, she most earnestly begged him to come again.

Penn then proceeded up the Rhine in his travels until he came to the Palatinate. There he tried to see the Elector of the Palatinate, the brother to Elizabeth. The Elector, too, had taken his stand for religious freedom, and had given an asylum to those of other faiths. When the Quaker Ames was compelled to flee from Neugier, the elector gave him an asylum. Indeed, Elizabeth had first learned to know about the Quakers from Ames, when at her brother's court in 1659. But Penn failed to meet the Elector.

After his return from England he again visited Princess Elizabeth at her home at Herford. He was again gladly received, and held meetings as before. But he now found there the Count of Dohna, one of the prominent nobles of the Brandenburg house. Dohna and he had soon got into a debate about the nature of Christianity and of conversion. They finally, however, agreed that self-denial was necessary. Penn then gave an account of his withdrawal from the world, when he became a Quaker. Dohna then attacked the peculiar custom of the Quakers in never lifting their hats, no, not even to kings. Penn tried to show him that such an act was "a weed of degeneracy, a mere fleshly honor," that it often covered insincerity, and that the hat should be lifted to no one but to God alone, when taken off in God's house. But Penn, notwithstanding the debate, held his services before the princess, and when he left, they invoked blessings on each other. After his departure she still continued to correspond with him. Her letters reveal her beautiful piety. She said: "My house and my heart are always open to those who love God." This correspondence between Penn and her was only broken by her death in 1680. Penn was greatly affected by it. He had a true regard for her. And two years after her death, when he published his second edition of his book, "No Cross, No Crown" (which he had written when imprisoned in the Tower of London), he perpetuated her memory by inserting her name there among the ancient and modern benefactors of mankind. He thus closes his eulogy on her: "She lived her single life till about 60 years of age, and then departed at her own house at Herwarden (Herford) as much lamented as she had lived—beloved by her people, to whose real worth I do with religious gratitude dedicate this memorial." This eulogy was written in the same year in which he sailed for America to administer his affairs here: so that it is evident that his first meeting with her was coincident with his first interest in America, and his last remarks about her were coincident with his going there. His relations to her were coincident with his relations to America, and prepared him to show special interest as he did later in our German Reformed forefathers who came to Pennsylvania in the eighteenth century. He felt he was returning a debt of gratitude to her by allowing her Church to be founded here. Our German Reformed Church here may thus be said to be a lasting memorial to Princess Elizabeth.

Penn visited her, hoping to make her a convert to the Quaker religion, but she ever remained an adherent to the Reformed faith of her childhood, although the inhabitants of her land were Lutherans. Her pietism offset the dangerous tendency of Descartes' philosophy toward rationalism. During her later years she still continued in correspondence with the leading thinkers of her age, such as Malebranche and Leibnitz. She seems to have exerted a remarkable influence in the progress of human thought. We have seen how Descartes' association with her and her family aided him to gain his influence in the world. Now again it was she who introduced Leibnitz to Malebranche's book in which he ventilates his views of correspondences, and tries to prove that his philosophy was in harmony with Christianity. Leibnitz carried this one step farther in his views of pre-existent harmony. She was always busy in aiding literature and science. She enriched the library of her abbey with many books. Her last days, however, were saddened as she saw her family was dying out, and there was danger of a Romish prince becoming ruler of the Palatinate. She died at Herford, February 11, 1680, aged sixty-two years. She was buried in the choir of the cathedral church at Herford, where the following epitaph is over her: "She bore a mind so truly royal, that amid all the reverses of fortune it remained unconquered. By her constancy and greatness of soul, by her singular prudence in the conduct of life, by her uncommon attainments in knowledge, by learning far above her sex, by the respect of kings and the friendship of the illustrious, by the correspondence and admiring tributes of the learned, by the united regard and applause of the whole Christian world, but chiefly by her own admirable virtue, she attached undying honor to her name."

ELECTRESS LOUISA HENRIETTA OF BRANDENBURG

VIII.

ELECTRESS LOUISA HENRIETTA OF BRANDENBURG.

A SAINT of the Reformed Church was Electress Louisa Henrietta of Brandenburg. What Miriam was among the Israelites, she was to the Reformed, the first sweet singer among the women of Israel. She was the author of the famous German hymn, "Jesus meine Zuversicht" (Jesus, my Redeemer, lives). She was a Dutch princess of the famous line of Orange, that ruled the Netherlands. She was born November 27, 1627, at the Hague in Holland, and was descended from the great families of William of Orange and Coligny. Her father, Count Frederick Henry of Orange-Nassau, had been governor of the Netherlands from 1625 to 1647. Her mother was a beautiful German princess, Countess Amalia of Solms. She was thus of noble blood, but made nobler by grace. Both of her parents were of the Reformed faith. Her mother, although French customs had become fashionable, yet did not think it beneath her to train her daughter in the mysteries of housekeeping. She also educated her with great care, and Louisa grew up tall, fair-haired and graceful. Her religious training she received from Rivet, a Reformed theologian. She loved to read the Bible and it became her constant companion. Many passages, especially from Isaiah, remained in her memory as the result of her early education.

When she was about eighteen years of age, the young Elector of Brandenburg, whose capital was at Berlin, was in western Germany busily watching the negotiations that closed the Thirty Years' War. And he also began negotiations of love, as well as of peace. As he had been reared partly in Holland, he knew her when a little girl, and had heard of her beauty as a young lady. This brave young prince therefore proposed to this beautiful princess, and was accepted. Of course there were difficulties in the way, for when did the course of true love run smooth? The Thirty Years' War had so impoverished his land, that he had to borrow 3000 thalers of his mother in order to be married. And Louisa, too, was restrained somewhat by her father's failing health. But the wedding nevertheless came off December 7, 1646, with great splendor, as was becoming princes of such high rank. The bride wore a costly dress of silver brocade, rich with Brabant lace.

A crown of brilliants and pearls adorned her head. The long train of her dress was carried by six ladies of noble birth. The Elector was not less elegantly dressed. He wore a vest and pants of white satin. The front of his vest was so full of diamonds that one could hardly discover the color of the cloth. There were many valuable presents made to them by relatives and foreign courts. A medal was struck which represented the young couple with joined hands.

But the bride did not go with her husband to Germany, on account of the ill health of her father. She remained faithfully with him until he died, three months after her wedding. After his death she accompanied her husband to Cleve in western Germany. Here her first child was born. The peace of Westphalia having closed the Thirty Years' War, the Elector in the autumn of 1648 started for his capital in eastern Germany. On the journey their child died at Wesel, to the great sorrow of the parents. The journey across Germany to Berlin lasted six months, and was a very sad one. It was sad to her because of the loss of her child. But it was made all the sadder because of the terrible devastation of the country through which they passed, caused by the awful Thirty Years' War. The roads were in a frightful condition, the fields were desolate, the people were poor and many of them starving. Their sufferings, added to her sorrows, made the journey very sad. But her sorrows only drove her closer to her Lord. They led her so near to Him, that they gave her the inspiration to write her immortal hymn, "Jesus, meine Zuversicht." Sad hearts sing sweetest songs. While on her journey, she rested for a month at Tangermunde, and there, probably, she composed that hymn:

> Jesus, my Redeemer, lives,
> Christ, my trust, is dead no more!
> In the strength this knowledge gives,
> Shall not all my fears be o'er;
> Calm, though death's long night be fraught
> Still with many an anxious thought?

The hymn is evidently based on the forty-sixth Psalm: "God is our refuge (Zuversicht) and strength," and also on Job 19:25, 27: "I know that my Redeemer liveth," and on I Corinthians 15. It was the expression of her confidence in God, which was the key to her life. It has been questioned whether she knew enough German to write such a hymn. But it is now well accepted that even though another hand may have polished it of its Hollandisms, yet the composition and the expression is hers. Runge, who published it for her, ascribes it to her. It has become one of the great Easter hymns of the German Church (for Gellert's great Easter hymn was not written till many years after), and is often sung at death-beds and funerals. It continues thus:

> Jesus, my Redeemer, lives,
> And His life I soon shall see;
> Bright the hope this promise gives;
> Where He is, I too shall be.
> Shall I fear Him? Can the head
> Rise and leave the members dead?
>
> Close to Him my soul is bound,
> In the bonds of hope enclasped;
> Faith's strong hand this hold hath found,
> And the Rock hath firmly grasped.
> Death shall ne'er my soul remove
> From her refuge in Thy love.
>
> I shall see Him with these eyes,
> Him whom I shall surely know,
> Not another shall I rise;
> With His love my heart shall glow;
> Only there shall disappear
> Weakness in and round me here.

Ye who suffer, sigh and moan,
Fresh and glorious there shall reign;
Earthly here the seed is sown,
Heavenly it shall rise again;
Natural here the death we die,
Spiritual our life on high.

Body, be thou of good cheer,
In thy Savior's care rejoice;
Give not place to gloom and fear,
Dead, thou yet shalt know His voice,
When the final trump is heard,
And the deaf, cold grave is stirred.

Laugh to scorn then death and hell,
Fear no more the gloomy grave;
Caught into the air to dwell
With the Lord who comes to save,
We shall trample on our foes,
Mortal weakness, fear and woes.

Only see ye that your heart
Rise betimes from earthly lust;
Would ye there with Him have part,
Here obey your Lord and trust.
Fix your hearts above the skies,
Whither ye yourselves would rise.

How grandly she rises over her sorrows in this hymn, and how sweetly she comforts others. This hymn has become historical. It became a favorite one in the royal family of Prussia. One of her successors, Queen Louisa, the good angel of Prussia at the beginning of this century and during the wars of Napoleon, was once standing before a picture of Electress Louisa Henrietta in the gallery at Charlottenburg, and she said: "The charming hymn has received citizenship in our Church and in all our families." And then, after being silent for a while, she sat herself down at the piano and sang it.

On the terrible night of March 18 and 19, 1848, when the German throne trembled in the throes of the Revolution, in the midst of the firing of guns and the thunder of artillery, over the wild tumult of the insurrection, the bells in the church tower at Potsdam played "Jesus, meine Zuversicht." It was a voice of comfort to many anxious hearts. And a few days later it again sounded forth from the castle, as 187 coffins of the fallen were escorted to their graves by 20,000 citizens. In the war of 1870 this hymn was a source of great comfort in the German army. The music books of many bands contained only two sacred tunes. One was "Nun danket alle Gott" (Now thank we all our God), and this hymn.

When Frederick William IV. of Prussia gave a

bell at the 200th anniversary of the founding of the orphanage at Oranienburg by the Electress Louisa Henrietta, he named the bell "Jesus, meine Zuversicht." And it had as its inscription the first two lines of the hymn. At the consecration of the bell the first verse of her hymn was sung.

Many other illustrations of the power and influence of this hymn might be given, to show how dear and sacred it has become to the German heart. When Ziegenbalg, the first of the German missionaries to go to the East Indies, lay dying, he called his friends to him, and in that distant land, as they stood around his bed, he asked them to sing "Jesus, meine Zuversicht." As they sang it, it gave him a look beyond the grave into heaven, and he said, "There is a light before my eyes as if the sun shone into my face." His spirit rose to heaven on the wings of that hymn. It is one of the great funeral hymns of the German language.

We will now look at her life more in detail. No wonder she could write such a hymn. Her pious life gave the inspiration for it. We left her at Tangermunde on her way to Berlin. After a month's rest she continued her journey with her husband until they arrived at Berlin, April 10, 1650. Here she was received with great joy by the people. But

Berlin, through the ravages of the Thirty Years' War, was a comparatively poor city of a few thousand inhabitants. Nevertheless her husband determined to make her comfortable. So he fitted up apartments in the palace on the side toward the river in Holland style; and also beautified the park before the palace with trees and flowers, even placing there, for her sake, some onion plants, so popular in Holland.

But she was not fond of the pomp of court life. Her tastes were simple, and her heart full of love to Christ. She preferred a quieter home, where she could meditate on her God. It happened, that while out hunting with her husband, she expressed herself as delighted with the location of an old hunting castle north of Berlin. Her kind husband, ever ready to satisfy her slightest wish, presented it to her, together with the neighboring district. He began building a castle there, which was finished in 1652. She then made this her home, and when she moved there, she gave it the name of Oranienburg (Orange-castle), naming it after her family, the family of Orange-Nassau. Here, separated from the world, she could live a quiet and religious life. This is the place which is associated especially with her life and works. She labored to make the district around the castle as productive as possible. She imported skilled gardeners from Holland, and founded quite a Dutch colony there. Among other things she introduced the cultivation of the potato from Holland, (this proved to be a great boon to the Germans, who had become so poor through the devastations of the Thirty Years' War), and soon the cultivation of the potato became universal. She was always doing good. She did not allow a single day to pass without doing some act of kindness to her people. The primary schools, which had been swept away by the war, she refounded. As a result she became a great favorite among the people. Many of the girls were named after her. As late as half a century ago, her name was a favorite one, and her portrait was still to be found on the walls of many farmers' houses. The following story of her kindness is told: On one occasion a servant stole something while she was at church. How did she punish him for his crime? She returned good for evil. When she learned of the theft, she gave him a goodly number of ducats and told him to get away as quickly as possible before her husband found it out. When her husband came and heard of the theft, he was very angry and said he would have hung the thief. To this she responded, "Even if all my gold and jewels were stolen, yet, if I had my way, not a drop of blood would be shed for it."

In this rural palace she lived in religious quietness. She was very diligent in her devotions. Much of her time was taken up in singing, reading of the Scriptures, and other religious exercises. She was always at church service. And it is said she made it a rule, never to look into a mirror before going to church, lest pride and fashion would disturb her thoughts. Her court preacher, Stosch, held many religious services in her palace. He was always welcome, and when he arrived he did not have to observe the usual rules of court etiquette and have himself announced, but could at once go to her apartments, as she was always glad to see him. Often she conversed with him on religious topics for three hours at a time. He bore a high testimony to her religious character. He said, "I have spent many hundred hours with her in private audience, talking to her about spiritual things." Indeed her room was more like a temple than a palace, for nothing that was not religious was allowed there. She always had morning and evening prayers.

Her health, however, was not good since the death of her first child. This was aggravated by anxiety for the future of her house. She feared lest if she had no heir, the house of Brandenburg would become Catholic, and terrible wars would result. This so preyed on her mind, that she finally went to her husband and suggested a divorce, an act which reveals her wonderfully self-denying character, for she was willing to sacrifice herself for the good of her land. But her noble husband refused, and a few years later God, in answer to her prayers, as to Hannah's, gave her a son. This son was born on a Tuesday, and ever after every Tuesday became a sacred day, for she spent it in fasting, prayer and thanksgiving, in commemoration of the event. In 1665 she opened an orphanage at Oranienburg, as a thank-offering for the gift of a son.

During the wars that followed, she was her husband's firm support and adviser. In spite of the rough roads and the dangers of the war, she went with him on his journeys. Thus during the Swedish war, when he had to go to Königsberg, she bravely went along, although the roads were in such a frightful condition that they could travel only eight miles in two days. The Swedes then forced the Elector to join them in war against Poland. The Poles, therefore, came and ravaged Brandenburg so fearfully, that no less than 31 towns were burned and 30,000 inhabitants murdered. These terrible events preyed on her mind, so that she could not sleep, and she suffered much from terrible dreams. During the war she cared for the spiritual condition of the soldiers, and ordered that a New Testament and Psalms be given to every soldier. When war with Sweden came again, she followed her husband into Pomerania, going with him even to the upper end of Jutland. She then went on a visit to western Germany, where she contracted a cold which produced a severe cough. She then went to her native land of Holland and felt better, but, although the weather was cold, she never gave up attending church. As she came out of church on March 14, she said to her lady in waiting, that she feared she might never live to get back to Berlin.

Finally after Easter she started for Berlin, because she wanted to see her husband and his children once more before she died. The journey was a long and rough one. She became weaker on the way. When she arrived at Hamm in Westphalia, she thought she would die, but prayed God most earnestly to spare her life that she might see her husband again at Berlin, and then she would say, "Now, Lord, lettest thou thy handmaiden depart in peace." Her prayer was granted. Her husband came to meet her as far as Halberstadt. The rest of the journey she had to make in a sedan chair. She was, however, greatly comforted all through the journey by the presence of Spanheim, one of the most renowned Reformed theologians of that time. He said of her, "Her patience is an example for us. Job and Jonah murmured; David cried out, 'How long, O Lord, how long,' but she never complained because of her weakness. She only complained that she gave so much trouble to others." One day he preached to her on the words, "God with us." She beautifully applied them to her own case. " 'God with us,' what a comfort in the sorrows of solitude, in dangerous waters, in the house of sorrow." At last she arrived at Berlin. Prayers were offered up in all the churches of the land for her recovery. But in spite of all the prayers for her dear life, her weakness became greater and greater. The Elector often watched beside her and comforted her by repeating Scripture texts. Not long before her death her chaplain asked her if she felt that God was gracious.

She answered, "Yes." That testimony was her last word, for she died soon after, on June 28, 1667. The whole land mourned her departure. Stosch preached her funeral sermon on Job 13:15, "Though He slay me, yet will I trust Him." She was greatly missed by the nation, but by none so much as by her husband, the Elector. For she had inherited the wisdom of a statesman from her ancestors, Coligny and William of Orange, and often had given him the best of advice in his political movements. After her death he was often found standing before her picture and crying out, "O Louisa, Louisa, if you were only with me with your counsels." Few princesses were so loved as she. Her memory still remains green among the German people. Nearly two hundred years after her death, the town of Oranienburg erected a monument to her. It is a life-size statue, standing on a granite pedestal nine feet high. Her head is adorned with a diamond. In her right hand is a roll—the manuscript of the founding of the orphanage there. Her earthly beauty and her heavenly piety made her one of the saints of the Reformed Church. Like Abel, she being dead, yet speaketh, for she has gained an earthly immortality through her hymn, as well as a heavenly immortality with her Savior.

Chapter II.—WOMEN OF OTHER LANDS.

I.

COUNTESS SUSAN RAKOCZY OF HUNGARY.

THE circle of Reformed princesses extended even to Hungary. The Hungarian Reformed Church was a martyr church and to-day is a strong denomination, containing over two million of adherents. The men and women who laid the foundations of that church in the 16th and 17th centuries were staunch Reformed, brave men and women, who feared not persecutions and loved their faith with all the intensity peculiar to the Magyar blood.*

Susan Lorantfy was born in 1600 at Saros-Patak, in Upper Hungary. Her father was descended from a noble Reformed family, and was possessed of large means. While he rejoiced at the birth of a daughter, he yet mourned that she was not a son, as he feared his line would die out and great complications arise through the Catholics. He confided his

---

* We are indebted for a sketch of this noble princess to a suggestion made by Rev. Prof. Balogh, of the Reformed Theological Seminary, of Debreczin, Hungary. At his request a sketch of her life was prepared by Rev. Stephen Verness, of Hungary, from which we gather our chapter on her life.

fears to the Reformed minister, who comforted him by saying that the best thing to do was to be submissive to God, accepting each gift from Him with great thankfulness. She had no joyous childhood, for her mother was not in good health and in giving birth to the next child, a daughter also, she died. Susan seldom saw her father, as he was busy with his widely-scattered worldly affairs and often absent from the home. There came over her a sadness, even a gloominess of disposition. Often she sat at the window, permitting her eyes to rove over room and garden, but nowhere finding the face of her dear mother, for whom she so greatly longed. These recollections made her mother seem to her as a guardian angel. Her only comfort was to cast her grief and loneliness on God in prayer or to divert herself from them by diligence in household arts, as spinning and sewing.

Her father then was married again to the bright and well-educated Catharine Andrassy, who cared for his children as if they were her own. Susan's training was mainly in the Word of God under the direction of the professors of the university at Saros-Patak. Thus the days of her childhood passed away until at the age of fifteen she lost also her father

Countess Susan Rakoczy of Hungary.

by death, and soon after her step-mother, too, who left a little daughter, Catharine, behind her: so that, young girl that she was, she had to be a mother to both her sister and her step-sister. These responsibilities deepened her nature and strengthened her faith. Much of her time was spent in study or in caring for the sick. The Reformed chaplain recommended to her support poor students at the College at Saros-Patak, to whom she gave generous support.

Then Prince George Rakoczy sued for her hand and they were married, April 18, 1616, and two years later his brother, Sigismund, married her sister, Maria. As the Rakoczy family was also strongly attached to the Reformed faith her home was very happy. But in 1619 trials began to come. Gabriel Bethlen, a noble of Transylvania, entered the Thirty Years' War and brought his army in the summer to Hungary. He reckoned on the help of young Rakoczy and was not disappointed, for George joined his forces. Susan, though she dreaded his absence, gave him the brave words, "Go, and God be with you. Go, and fight for your God, religion and Fatherland." The unfortunate war soon compelled him to return and peace followed. She then devoted herself to the training of her four children, who attended the college for their education. This college was her greatest care, for she recognized that education was necessary to lay permanent foundations for piety. How beautiful it is, for woman to be the patroness of learning. She saw to it that the best teachers were found for this institution and to this end she called Amos Comenius, the famous teacher, who undertook the thorough organization of the college. He remained there four years, at a yearly salary of 6,000 gulden (2,400 dollars), and laid the foundations of the future for that university. She and her husband were regular attendants at the Reformed service. He was a great student of the Bible, which he read through a number of times. When any great discussions took place on religious subjects by the pastors of Saros-Patak he was always present and often took part himself. Before he ever went on a journey, he always had a church service, and when he returned he quickly sought the house of prayer to thank God for his safe return.

In 1630, as Gabriel Bethlen had died and left no male heir, George Rakoczy was elected by Translyvania as his successor. This compelled his removal to its capital, Gyulafehervar. Here, again, Susan became the patroness of the college. She often expressed her views to the ministers who visited her, and was led to publish a theological work on "Moses and the Prophets." This caused much unpleasantness. That a woman should appear publicly in a theological work caused no little sensation. The Catholics sharply criticized it. And her husband was so angered that the Jesuit who did so barely escaped his wrath. Their sons, in the meantime, were educated and confirmed in the Reformed church at the capital, at which time they produced their personal confessions of faith, which so stirred all that tears of joy were shed.

Countess Susan once had an unpleasant experience as the result of her benefactions. It had been her custom, not only to support many students at the university of Saros-Patak, but also to annually give money to students of talent that they might prosecute their studies in foreign lands. But the young men who went to England became adherents of the Presbyterial form of church government. And they tried on their return to introduce it into their own Reformed church in Hungary, which had superintendents called bishops. The Countess, although princes generally favored bishops, herself favored the Presbyterial order. This, however, brought her into conflict with prominent ministers of her own church, who favored the other system. Some of the adherents of the Presbyterial idea were driven away and she herself had the humiliation of being held back from the Lord's Supper by the church which she had so royally supported. But she forgave all and called together conferences, which finally healed the strife. About the same time the Catholics began persecuting the Reformed and taking away their churches. Count Rakoczy took up arms for them and came home victorious, having gained religious liberty for the Reformed of Hungary, after having humiliated the Emperor by peace and freedom. Her husband died some time after the war, and her son George came to the throne. Susan then returned from Gyulafehervar, the capital of Transylvania, to her old home at Saros-Patak, where she spent her last years in caring for the church and the university. Here her second son and his wife died, while her other son only brought political trouble on her land, and finally also died. Alone she was left, with only God to help and comfort. Death came to her, April 18, 1661, as she awaited it with joy and quietness. She is a fine illustration of what women of wealth can do for the Lord by their influence and means. She will ever live in Hungarian history as the patroness of the Church and the university, and we are glad to tell her fame and her goodness to other nations and churches who knew not of her.

HUGUENOT WOMEN OF THE TOWER OF CONSTANCE

II.

THE WOMEN OF THE TOWER OF CONSTANCE IN FRANCE.

THE Huguenot Church has been famous for its martyrs, but among them none are more noble than the women. We have given a brief sketch of one of them in the previous century, Philippine of Luns. There is one place that is especially associated with the female martyrs of the French Reformed Church. It is the tower of Constance at Aigues-Mortes in southern France, not far from the Mediterranean. There, it is true, they did not die, but they suffered worse,—theirs was a living death as they were imprisoned for life. The tower consisted of two large circular apartments, one above the other. The lower one received light only from the other, through a round hole about six feet in diameter. The upper is pierced by a similar aperture in the center of a vaulted ceiling, beneath the terrace that covers the tower. By these apertures alone can smoke escape, or the fresh air enter, and with the air cold, rain and wind.

When the Revocation of the Edict of Nantes in 1585 made it unlawful for the Reformed to worship in France, the galleys on the Mediterranean became the prison for the ministers and the men, and this tower, for the women. It was well-named the Tower of Constance or of constancy, for they remained firm and constant to their Reformed faith in spite of their sufferings. Their only crime had been that they had attended a Reformed service in the woods or in caves, or had sent their children there. And yet for this they were virtually entombed alive. In it they were continually solicited to give up their faith. Priests and laymen, foreigners and Frenchmen urged them to kiss the crucifix so as to become free. But no, they would not. Twenty-five women were confined there, according to the list given by Marie Durand in 1754. One of them, Marie Berand, was blind, but in spite of her blindness she was seized, by order of the king, torn from her home and conveyed to the tower where she died, aged 80 years. Another, Marie Rey, had been separated from her children because she had taken part in a Reformed service. She was detained a prisoner since 1737. A third, Marie Neviliard, was separated from her children because she had been married by a Reformed minister, which was illegal, according to the law. The following story is told of a fourth. At the end of March, 1735, in the plain of Bruzac, a Protestant service was being held for the celebration of the Lord's Supper. Suddenly the congregation was broken into by soldiers and all who were not able to escape were arrested, among them a young couple, Francis Fiale and his wife, Isabeau Menet. He was condemned to the galleys either at Marseilles or Toulon, where he died in 1743. His wife was cast into the tower of Constance, where she gave birth to a child, which was taken away from her to be reared a Catholic. Her letters tell the sad story of the sufferings of the long captivity, of the sorrow of separation from her child, and of the death of her husband. Though sad, they are full of hope and piety. Nowhere do they breathe any trace of anger against her persecutors.

But the most interesting and best-known of the captives was Marie Durand. She entered the prison a young girl of 15; she left it an old woman, aged 53, white with gray hairs. Her story was that as the French officers had not been able to catch her brother, one of the most zealous of the French Reformed ministers, who secretly held services, they took her aged father in his place, and imprisoned him until he died. And then the French commandant determined to try it on his daughter, only fifteen years of age. She was to be imprisoned for her brother's activity. As she was superior in education to most of the women in the tower (who belonged to the artisan class), she soon gained the confidence of the sad colony and became their interpreter and correspondent. She corresponded, especially in the later years, when the surveillance was less strict, with Paul Rabaut, the famous French preacher of the Desert, and others. We once heard Rev. Mr. Bersier, of Paris, tell the story that he had a glove-psalter,—that is a hymn-book such as the French ladies could hide in their gloves. "This glove-psalter," he said, "I can never touch without emotion, for it belonged to a girl who was arrested at the age of fifteen for having gone to worship in the mountains, and who was shut up in the famous tower of Constance, where she remained forty years: and where one winter's night she had her foot half-eaten by a rat. There, on those pages, you can clearly see the traces of her tears, chiefly on some of the Psalms, such as the 42d, where David says he will once more go to the tabernacle of the Lord and sing his praises in the great congregation."

In 1764 the register of Aigues-Mortes announced

to them that the Jesuits had been driven out of France and that religious liberty was granted in France, but that they would be retained in prison until their death, because most of them were aged and infirm, and as it was not possible to return their confiscated property. At this they were plunged in the greatest consternation, so that they all became sick. In their agony they charged Marie Durant to write to Paul Rabaut, who appealed to the various members of the nobility to aid them. It was the prince of Beauveau who was mainly instrumental in gaining their freedom. While near the tower on business he determined to visit it. He says they were conducted up an obscure and winding stairs to a large round room deprived of air or of the light of day. There they found fourteen women languishing in misery. As he looked at them he could not control his feelings. They fell at his feet, overpowered with weeping, so that they could not at first speak, and when speech came, they all together recounted their common sufferings. He was interested by the story of Gabrielle Guinges, who had given two sons to die in the French wars, yet was permitted to languish in prison. He was touched by the miserable appearance of Jeanne Auguiere and Isabeau Maumejan, who were eighty years of age, and of Isabeau Anne Gaussaint, of Sommieres, who was ninety years, and who had been imprisoned for 36 years.

Overcome by a noble instinct of compassion, he himself broke the chains of their sufferings and gave them their liberty. For this he was threatened with the loss of his office. He replied in fiery words, "The king is my master to deprive me of my place, but not to prohibit me from fulfilling my duties to my conscience and my honor." The prisoners quitted their sad abode. But where could they go? Their property had been confiscated. Their friends were dead. Marie Durand was able to return to her former home, now in ruins. The consistory of Amsterdam hearing of her sufferings and poverty gave her a life-pension of 200 livres. But the flower of their life was gone, given for their faith. Yet "the blood of the martyrs is the seed of the Church." Not far from the tower there is now a modest Reformed chapel, where every Sunday the Reformed meet to the number of 150. This church (or temple, as they call Protestant churches in France), was dedicated February 22, 1863.

Let this tower of Constance be an inspiration to

the women of our Church today, that they may be constant in their faith. There is no persecution now and yet there is what is worse, a worldliness that silently saps all piety. O, if the women of the tower of Constance could remain true to their faith in spite of such persecutions for so many years, what an inspiration it ought to be to the ladies of our Church today to be true to their Reformed churches. May the faithfulness of these martyrs prove an inspiration to nobleness and firmness of character in all who read this book.

PART III.
Women of the Eighteenth and Nineteenth Centuries.

CHAPTER I.—WOMEN OF SWITZERLAND.

I.
ANNA LAVATER.

"WHY have I heard so little of the noble Anna Lavater?" once wrote a friend of her husband. "I find so much that is grand and noble in this excellent woman, which I can find only among the truly godly." Let us hear more about this noble life.

Anna Schinz, for such was her maiden name, was born July 8, 1742, at Zurich. She had a deeply religious mother, and she early revealed a very pious disposition. Once a companion, whom she had been forbidden to associate with, tempted her to go away with her. She did so; but when she came back, her flushed countenance betrayed a guilty conscience. "My child," said the mother, "I see you have done something wrong." She confessed the fault with tears. Then her wise mother said: "Anna, we will not talk together; come, let us pray." And she led her to a room, where they were alone with God, and there they prayed. Happy is the child that has such a pious mother to take her to the throne of grace. She also showed great kindness of heart. A female laborer, well-known to the family, had become so disabled that she came into great want. Little Anna delighted to minister to her. Whenever she would have something nice to eat, she would lay aside a part of it and take it to this poor invalid. Often, rather than spend an hour in the evening in the company of her companions, she would go to this aged friend. And as she did not want to go empty-handed, if she had nothing else, she would take her own evening meal to her friend.

She was also very fond of nature and also of her Bible. In the palace garden she used to have a favorite place under the shadow of a tree beside a waterfall, where there was a wide view; for in Thurgau (whither her father removed soon after her birth) there is fine scenery. There she loved to take out her New Testament and read and pray. One day a younger brother surprised her by building a little house there, so that she could sit in it when the weather was unpleasant. In it he placed a table made by himself, and on it lay her Bible. This prayer-place became a blessing and an inspiration to her life. Many years after, when old and gray, a lady friend brought her a flower plucked from it. The little flower brought tears to her eyes, as she remembered what that sacred place had done for her. Thus, with love to God, nature and her fellow-men, she grew up, and by it was prepared for her life-work before her.

On May 6, 1766, Rev. Casper Lavater sued for her hand. A few years before, in a letter to a friend, he describes the kind of person who was his ideal of a wife: "She must have a good heart, for of the most importance is her moral character. She must, therefore, be mild, quiet and modest. She need not be beautiful, if she is only pleasant, healthful, neat and gentle. She must understand well domestic management, although it is not necessary for her to be learned—a pedant I detest. She must be teachable, compliant and determined to assist and not to hinder me in my official duties. She must aid me in my labors in visiting the sick." We presume he found these qualifications in Anna Schinz, whom he married June 3, 1766. She thus became the wife of the most brilliant of the young ministers of Zurich, and one of the most famous men of his time. Her married life was very happy, although clouded at times by the death of children.

In April, 1769, her husband was made assistant pastor of the Orphans Home church at Zurich. This position imposed on him the duty, in addition to his other pastoral labors, of caring for the orphan children and for the convicts in the prison. In these spheres he found in his wife a zealous help-meet. It happened, too, that the next two years were years of famine. Great was the suffering of the hungry people, as they surged through the streets in crowds. Her house became a place for the distribution of alms to the poor. Here she again revealed her great kindness of heart. She always kept a kettle of warm soup on the fire to be given to the poor. One day the door-bell rang, and she saw through the window a poor man, hardly able to stand. She hurried to him, but he had already fallen to the ground, before she came to him. She helped him to a chair and gave him warm soup. But seeing his great weakness, she hastened into the house for a glass of wine, when suddenly he died from the weakness caused by the starvation. On another occasion she started out on a walk with her husband. They had gone but a very short distance, when they found a poor woman sitting on the ground, trying to quiet her little babe. When asked what was the matter, she replied, with tears in her eyes, that she had only one request to make, and that was that God would soon release herself and her child from their hunger, by letting them die. For she had had nothing to eat, and so could not give her child anything. Of course Mr. and Mrs. Lavater's walk was at an end. They took the woman and the child home with them, and after giving her food, had her name entered on the poor list, so that she received money weekly out of the charity fund.

It was the usual practice of Mr. Lavater to read every morning several chapters in the Bible, and to select from them one particular passage for frequent and special meditation during the day. One morning, after reading the fifth and sixth chapters of St. Matthew, he exclaimed, "What a treasure of morality! How difficult to make choice of any portion of it!" After a few minutes' consideration, he threw himself on his knees and prayed for divine guidance. When he joined his wife at dinner she asked him what passage of Scripture he had chosen for the day. "Give to him that asketh thee, and from him that would borrow of thee turn not thou away," was the reply.

"And how is this to be understood?"

" 'Give to him that asketh thee, and from him that would borrow of thee turn thou not away,' are the words of Him," rejoined Mr. Lavater, "to whom all and everything belongs that I possess. I am the steward, not the proprietor. The proprietor desires me to give to him that asks me, and not to refuse him who would borrow of me, or, in other words, if I have two coats, I must give to him who has none; and if I have food, I must share with him who is an hungered and in want. This I must do without being asked; how much more, then, should I do so when asked?"

"This," continues Mr. Lavater in his diary, "appeared to me so evidently and undoubtedly to be the meaning of the verses in question, that I spoke with more than usual warmth. My wife made no further reply than that she would take these things to heart.

"I had scarcely left the dining-room a few minutes when an aged widow desired to speak with me, and she was shown into my study. 'Forgive me, dear sir,' she said; 'excuse the liberty I am about to take. I am truly ashamed, but my rent is due tomorrow, and I am short of six dollars. I have been confined to my bed by sickness, and my poor child is nearly starving. Every penny that I could save I have laid aside to meet this demand, but six dollars are yet wanting and tomorrow is term-day.'

"Here she opened a parcel which she held in her hand, and said: 'This is a book with a silver clasp, which my late husband gave me the day we were married. It is all I can spare of the few articles I possess, and how it grieves me to part with it! I am aware that it is not enough, nor do I see how I could ever repay you; but, dear sir, if you can, do assist me!'

"'I am very sorry, my good woman, that I cannot help you,' I said; and, putting my hand into my pocket, I accidently felt my purse, which contained about two dollars. These, I said to myself, can not extricate her from her difficulty—she requires six; besides, if even they could, I have need of this money for some other purpose. Turning, then, to the widow, I said: 'Have you no friend, no relation who could give you this trifle?'

"'No, not a soul! I am ashamed to go from house to house. I would rather work day and night. My excuse for being here is that people speak so much of your goodness. If, however, you can not assist me, you will at least forgive my intrusion, and God, who has never yet forsaken me, will not surely turn away from me in my sixty-sixth year.'

"At this moment the door of my apartment opened, and my wife entered. I was ashamed and vexed, and gladly would I have sent her away, for conscience whispered, 'Give to him that asketh thee, and from him that would borrow of thee turn not thou away.' She came up to me and said with much sweetness, 'This is a good old woman; she has certainly been ill of late; assist her if you can.'

"Shame and compassion struggled in my darkened soul. 'I have but two dollars,' I said in a whisper, 'and she requires six. I will give her a trifle and let her go.'

"Laying her hand on my arm, and smilingly looking into my face, my wife said aloud what conscience whispered before, 'Give to him that asketh thee, and from him that would borrow of thee turn not thou away.'

"I blushed and replied with some little vexation, 'Would you give your ring for that purpose?'

"'With pleasure,' answered my wife, pulling off her ring.

"The good old woman was either too simple or too modest to notice what was going on, and was preparing to retire, when my wife called to her to wait in the hall. When we were left alone I asked my wife, 'Are you in earnest about the ring?'

"'Certainly, how can you doubt it?' she said. 'Do you think I would trifle with charity? Remember what you said to me but half an hour ago! O, my dear, let us not make a show of the gospel! You are in general so kind, so sympathizing; how is it that you find it so difficult to assist this poor woman? Why did you not, without hesitation, give her what you had in your pocket? And did you not know that there were yet six dollars in your desk, and that your quarter's salary will be paid to us in less than eight days?

"She then added, with much feeling, 'Take no thought for your life, what ye shall eat, or what ye shall drink; nor yet for your body, what ye shall put on. Behold the fowls of the air: they sow not neither do they reap, nor gather into barns; yet your heavenly Father feedeth them.'

"I kissed my wife, while tears ran down my cheeks. 'Thanks, a thousand thanks for this humiliation! I turned to the desk, took from it the six dollars, and opened the door to call in the poor widow. All darkened around me at the thought that I had been so forgetful of the omniscience of God as to say to her, 'I cannot help you.' O, thou false tongue—thou false heart! If the Lord should mark iniquities, O. Lord, who shall stand?

"'Here is what you need,' I said, addressing the widow.

"At first she seemed not to understand what I meant, and thought I was offering her a small contribution, for which she thanked me, and pressed my hand; but, when she perceived that I had given her the whole sum, she could scarcely find words to express her feelings. She cried, 'Dear sir, I can not repay you; all I possess is this book, and it is old.'

"'Keep your book,' I said, 'and the money, too, and thank God, and not me, for verily I deserve no thanks after having so long resisted your entreaties. Go in peace, and forgive an erring brother.'

"I returned to my wife with downcast looks, but she smiled, and said, 'Do not take it so much to heart, my dear; you yielded at my first suggestion. But promise me that so long as I wear a gold ring on my finger—and you know that I possess several besides—you will never allow yourself to say to any poor person, 'I cannot help you.' She then kissed me, and left the apartment."

We will mention but one remarkable occurrence that took place in that year, and which proves, at least, how fully Mr. Lavater and his wife, even when they were widely separated from each other, were united to each other by the bond of devoted Christian love. During the month of August Mr. Lavater visited his friend Dr. Holtze, who lived in the charming town of Richterswyl, on Lake Zurich. Shortly after his arrival he wrote to his wife that he was enjoying perfect health. On the following day, however, when Mrs. Lavater was sitting alone in her husband's room, she suddenly became so overpowered by anxiety for him that she could scarcely move. Recovering herself, she went to her father-in-law and told him of her state of mind.

The affectionate father consoled her with friendly and cheering words, urging her that, since she had good news from her husband only the day before, she must attach no importance to her gloomy feelings. As long as her venerable father was urging her to cast aside her fears, she felt somewhat cheerful, but when she returned to Mr. Lavater's room again, the same anxiety took possession of her mind, and she fell upon her knees, weeping and praying.

At this very hour Mr. Lavater's life was in a very

perilous situation. He had left Richterswyl, and was on his way to visit a friend who lived on the other side of Lake Zurich, at Oberried. When he went into the little boat, which was to convey him to the place, the wind and water were very calm. Gradually a fresh wind arose, which impelled the boat very rapidly, and just as they reached the most dangerous point of the lake, the wind increased to a storm. The storm grew to a hurricane, and the waves rolled higher and higher, every moment threatening to overturn the boat. The boatmen, who had had much experience, and were generally fearless, exclaimed, with despairing voices, "We shall go down! Down with the sails! Hold, for God's sake! Back with the sail! Away! Away! She strikes! We are lost! We are gone!"

The mast of the little boat was entirely shattered by the storm. The boatmen then exclaimed, "We can do nothing more!" Mr. Lavater was upon his knees praying, thinking of death, of his wife and children. From his innermost soul he prayed God to have compassion on him and his associates in danger, and deliver them from this fearful storm. At the same hour his wife was in his room at home, wrestling and praying for his deliverance. God heard and answered their prayers. One can imagine Mrs. Lavater's feelings on meeting her husband after the fearful presentiment she had of his death, and the tears of joy she shed at having him once more restored to her and the children. She united with him, from the depths of her soul, in praising God for so wonderfully delivering him. So was the grief of an hour, through the mercy of God, turned into thankfulness and joy.

Her husband became to her a constant source of anxiety and care. He had never been strong, having a predisposition to consumption. After a few years of severe labor at the Orphans Home church, his health broke down, and he went to Germany to the baths. During his absence she had to bear all the cares of the family herself, even to nursing and burying a little son during his absence. He returned, and in 1778 was elected to one of the most prominent positions in the canton, namely, pastor of the St. Peter's church, at Zurich. As this parish had more than 5000 souls, it meant more work for him and also for her. Finally came the most trying of all experiences to her as a faithful wife. The ominous French Revolution broke out. And when the French proceeded to occupy Switzerland, her husband was one of the few who openly attacked them. When the Helvetic Directory oppressed the Swiss, he openly lifted up his voice in their defence. He wrote against them his "Word of a Free Swiss to a Great Nation." And he preached against them in his pulpit, April 7, 1799.

For this his life was in the greatest danger. So when he and his wife had gone to the baths for his health (for he was again suffering from rheumatism) on May 16, at six A. M. there was a rap at his door. According to his custom, he exclaimed, "Come in!" Although the sufferer was lying in bed, three men came in and communicated to him the fact that they had been commissioned by the Directory of the Helvetic Republic to take possession of all his papers. Mr. Lavater quietly answered, "Now, in God's name, take what you find, and discharge your duty!" Thereupon one of the three men, the Prefect Tobler, showed him the written order requiring his transportation immediately to Basle. Mr. Lavater likewise received this message calmly, with undisturbed mien, and replied quietly, "I have nothing to say to this either. I will put up with whatever you do. However, bear in mind my diseased condition." Mrs. Lavater, who could not endure the scene quietly any longer, then said, "What, would you take my sick husband away from the very place where he has come to get a little strength? No, I don't believe you can. I can not let him go away. You can watch him here all you please, for he will not attempt to escape from you. To take him away, in his present state, would be—I, at least, can not submit to it."

Mr. Lavater then found it necessary, first of all, to calm his wife, for he saw that she was greatly excited. He then said to her, "Let God's will be done! You see that I must go through with this. Let it be. Be quiet, for that is the best course. You are too frail to endure the journey, and would be of no service to me. Return at once from Baden to Zurich. Be assured that God will give me friends wherever I go. He will do everything for the benefit of my health. I shall want nothing. God will be as near to me in Basle as in Baden or in Zurich. Take courage, and submit to circumstances. It is God's will, as you very well see. Though you are certain of my innocence, you can be equally assured that God will not forsake me, and will not prevent my innocence from being proved to the world. Certainly, I should have learned very little, if I had not learned to trust God fearlessly and in a child-like way under such circumstances. Good-bye, we shall soon meet again."

After having said this, Mr. Lavater turned to the Prefect again, and said to him, "I urge upon you to think if I am really ready for the undertaking, and whether it is really prudent to visit upon an innocent and sick man, and upon a public teacher, in this time of trouble, such measures of violence as you propose to inflict upon me. And as far as I am concerned, I am perfectly ready to obey your orders. But I assure you, further, that I have spent half of last night in excruciating pain, and that I have only expected relief by means of the waters of this place."

The Prefect answered, "I believe it is true that you preached on the 13th of May. However, can you say that it is physically impossible for you to leave the bed?"

Mr. Lavater replied, "I can not say that such is the fact, for I came from Zurich to Baden the day before yesterday, though with great difficulty; but since I have reached here, my pain has increased."

The three men retired from the room for a moment to consult together as to what was best to be done. They soon returned, and then the Prefect said, "I can not allow you to remain here; I must carry out my orders."

"Now, in God's name," replied Mr. Lavater, "let His will be done!"

The officers at once secured the sick man's papers, and transported him to Basle. The three deputies were not even kind-hearted enough to leave him and his wife alone for a moment, and her earnest entreaties to be permitted to accompany her husband were inexorably rejected. They were treated as if they were both heinous offenders. Mrs. Lavater, however, was enabled to contribute an important service to her husband and to the good cause which he loved. In a wardrobe in the room there was a large portfolio containing loose writing and important letters of friends. Among them all there was not a syllable which a pure heart could misinterpret as dangerous to the State. Still, in case any of them were to fall into the hands of his enemies, they might be perverted into testimony against him.

Mrs. Lavater thought of this, and as she passed toward a corner of the room, she stood for a moment at the door of the wardrobe, and, unperceived by any one, even her husband, she locked the door, and handed the key to a servant-girl who was standing near by. In this way the very existence of a closet was not observed, for it was made in the wall, and it would not have been very easy to detect it without a knob or a key to show its whereabouts. As already intimated, the thoughtfulness of Mrs. Lavater proved, in the end, very well-timed, for it was afterward found that among the papers were some of the very greatest importance to Mr. Lavater.

But the hardest trial of all to her life was the wounding and death of her husband. On the 26th of September, 1799, the French captured Zurich, and her husband, while standing in front of his house, was shot by a French soldier, whom he had befriended a few moments before. Suffering severe pain, he was brought into the house, to suffer often intensest agony for more than a year, until he died, January 2, 1801. During all that time she was his constant companion, his faithful nurse and strong support— a model minister's wife. He died blessing her for what she had done for him.

Thus their happy married life of thirty-five years was broken up, and she entered on the sad years of widowhood and old age. She now centered her life in the care of her children and grandchildren. On Easter, 1811, she was seized with a severe fever and remained weak for a year. Her face became so pale and thin that she could scarcely look at herself in the glass. But she said: "O how rejoiced I am that I have a merciful Savior, to whom I can unite in heart and soul and be at rest." Finally after some years of ill health, March 28, 1815, she called her grandchildren to her and embraced them, saying: "So may our Lord Jesus embrace you in His arms, as I do now in my dying arms." She still lived till September 24, when her spirit fled from its clay tent to its Lord. Her character is beautifully described in the following tribute: "She was so beloved by every one, because she forgot herself in her love for God and man. Hence her fidelity to her mission, her silent patience in sorrow, her purity, beneficence and wonderful charity."

II.
ANNA SCHLATTER AND META HEUSSER-SCHWEITZER.

TWO Swiss saints are these two Christian women, worthy of perpetual remembrance in the Reformed Church. The first lived in the canton of St. Gall, the second in the canton of Zurich, but they were close friends, and may, therefore, be sketched together.

Anna Schlatter was born at St. Gall, November 5, 1773, the next to the youngest sister among twelve children. She was the daughter of a prominent manufacturer and citizen, named Bernet. Her lot had fallen in hard times, for in her girlhood her family had to struggle financially, and in her maturity she had to contend against the prevailing Rationalism. Yet she stood as a witness for the truth—a modern Reformed Miriam, singing her poetic songs when the Church was threatened, not by the hosts of Egypt, as in Miriam's time, but by unbelief. Fortunately for her, her family was a pious one. One of her ancestors had been the reformer of St. Gall—Watt or Vadianus. She was, therefore, reared under spiritual influences. On Sunday she was trained to go regularly to church, and, according to the custom of the times, she was not allowed to take a walk till after afternoon service. There came a famine to the land, and many of the people suffered much from hunger. Her father's business declined, and he was compelled to give it up when she was three years of age. Suddenly he died, April 26, 1800, when she was seven years old. After her father's death she clung closer than ever to her mother, but it was not long. A year later her mother, in the midst of her children at the table, after she had said grace, suddenly had a stroke and died. Left an orphan, she was cared for by the orphans' God. And although those were days of unbelief, yet God led her to Himself. A sermon by Haseli, read when she was thirteen years old, deeply convicted her of her sins, and led her to come to God in deepest penitence. She was confirmed at the age of fifteen. But the catechetical instruction of the city pastor, Stahelin, seemed cold to her earnest heart. She longed for a warmer, higher religious experience and life. Fortunately for her, she became associated with Lavater's family, and this led her ultimately to full assurance of salvation. In 1792 she learned to know Nette, Levater's daughter, who afterwards became the wife of Antistes Gessner, of Zurich. Through her she learned to know Lavater. She read his books, from which she derived much comfort and light. And when Lavater visited St. Gall in 1793, she visited him and put to him the great questions of her soul. He pointed her to God, and she was satisfied. She thus inclined toward the Pietism, rather than the rationalism, of her day.

In that year Hector Schlatter, a prominent citizen of St. Gall, proposed marriage. Many and deep were her conflicts. She loved him, but he was a rationalist like his uncle Zollikofer, the great pulpit-orator of Leipsic. Did not the Bible forbid an unequal yoking together of believers with unbelievers? She went to God in prayer. And on her knees she prayed to God to put some hindrance in the way of their marriage, if it was going to influence her away from Him. Lavater, too, gave his advice that she marry him. And Mr. Schlatter promised never to interfere with her religious views. So hoping to lead him to a saving knowledge of Jesus, she married him February 18, 1794, Antistes Scherrer preaching the marriage sermon on Psalm 103:17, 18. After their marriage she remained true to her Church, although touched somewhat by worldliness. But in 1804 there came a change. She names February 22 of that year as the day of her completed assurance. On that day she says, "I gave myself entirely without any exception, with all that I am and have, living and dying, to Him. And the peace of God higher than all knowledge filled my soul. I was a new creature. Everything appeared to me in a different light. Prayer was my delight, the reading of the Bible my highest pleasure, and the Gospel was to me a treasure, whose key I never before had had." She now labored and prayed more earnestly than ever for the conversion of her husband. He never read the Bible, and although he prayed, yet it was about earthly things. To spiritual truths his soul was dark. She continued in prayer for him, but it was not until the death of his father that he softened and said to his wife, "How thankful I am that among Christ's disciples there was a doubting Thomas." His wife, quick to discern her opportunity, said to him, "Yes, but Jesus said to Thomas, 'Blessed are they who not having seen yet believe.'" With joy she now noticed that he read his Bible. And the more he read the more he saw that his own morality could not save him, until finally she had the great joy of seeing him an humble follower of Christ. Thus by her piety she sanctified the unbelieving husband, and by her prayers brought him to Christ. What an encouragement this to wives praying for unsaved husbands.

Many, however, were her cares and anxieties as mother. Thirteen children came to bless her home. But she had a great mother-heart to take them all in. Nevertheless they brought many cares. In all she was as careful a housekeeper as a loving mother. No article of clothing, no bed clothes, not even a stocking failed to pass her close inspection. She was seamstress, washerwoman and everything else in her home. Many sorrows came to her in these cares. Three children died in early childhood, two of them within a quarter of an hour of each other. Yet, in spite of all these cares and troubles, she found time to write the most beautiful poems. And while excelling as a housekeeper in industry, economy and executive ability, she also excelled as a writer of religious hymns and letters. Her religious prose is classic in its style. But it was especially as "mother" that her piety appears in her writings. She had great love for children, and her great desire was to train them all for God. Her mother-words are wonderful. Exquisitely beautiful are her words of advice to her son at his confirmation in 1810, entitled,

"Words of a warm mother-heart laid on a tender child's heart." And very touching are her words to her daughter at confirmation in 1815. And to one of her sons, who was on a journey, she wrote, "Some mother-words for a traveler's pocket." Surely no son could go astray with such a letter in his pocket. No wonder that with such a mother (for not all sons have such a mother) one of her sons, Casper, became a minister.

The first of her writings to be published was her letter to her oldest son on his confirmation day, 1810. It was published without her knowledge by a friend, Engelman, at Stuttgard, in 1817. Her writings were so beautiful and loving, so chaste and artless, that they gave her fame. Knapp published eleven of her hymns in 1837. Her poems were published in 1835, and the next year another edition was required. One hundred and thirty-two of her hymns and poems have been printed, some of them masterpieces.

But great as is her fame as a poetess, as her son-in-law, Zahn, says very beautifully, her greater fame is her "mother fame." We regret that not more of her beautiful poems and hymns have found their way into English. Her confirmation hymn, written in her letter to her son on confirmation day, 1810, is worthy of a place in our hymnology. Thus, by her writings, Anna Schlatter became the centre of an awakening in the beginning of the century, and exerted an influence far beyond her family and her land. She had a large correspondence with leading theological thinkers of her time, as Lavater at Zurich, Yung Stilling at Heidelberg, Menken at Bremen, the Quaker Grellet as New York, and others, and even with evangelical Catholics, as Sailor, Boos, Gossner, and others. Noble people corresponded with her or visited her. In 1821 she made one distant trip to Barmen, Germany, where she was delighted with the religious life of the Reformed Wupperthal. She also developed great activity, especially in the circulation of the Bible among the Catholics. She started the cause of missions in her canton and gave her son, Casper, as one of the teachers of the newly-founded mission house at Basle. After a visit of pastor Steinkopf, of London, to St. Gall, she became so enthusiastic on the subject of missions that she organized a woman's missionary society at her house. Thus a Reformed poetess is the founder of the first Women's Missionary Society in Europe, just as a Reformed lady, Mrs. Doremus, was the founder of ladies' missionary societies in

America. She also raised a good deal of money among her friends for missions.

Her last years were years of great suffering, as she had to lie in bed with dropsy. But God's grace was sufficient for her. She became so happy at the thought of death that she did not want to hear her friends suggest to her the possibility of a recovery. She died February 25, 1826. Her last words were, "God is mine and I am His."

Sweet as were the poet songs of Anna Schlatter, still sweeter were the strains of her Reformed sister, Meta Heusser-Schweitzer. "The most beautiful religious poetess of the German language," once said Dr. Schaff to me. She was about a quarter of a century younger than Anna Schlatter, and was born April 6, 1797. The place of her birth, Hirzel, in canton Zurich, continued to be the scene of her life till her death. It is a beautiful hilltop overlooking the Zurich lake on the north, and to the east and south, the snow-capped Alps. In this quiet mountain parish her father was pastor for many years, till he died in 1824. Here she grew up in absolute quietness and retirement, never going away from it till she was about sixteen years of age. Her first trip was made to St. Gall, where she came into contact with the family of Anna Schlatter, and formed a very close attachment with her daughter, with whom she kept up correspondence until death. In 1821 she married Dr. Heusser, the physician of her home, Hirzel.

> "Her's was woman's usual lot,
> Cares and trials wanting not."

She had seven children and cares enough to make life very prosaic, but her natural poetic genius leaped over all barriers and burst forth in sweetest song. Her greatest cares made her sing the sweetest. "As a bird sings among the branches, so she sang." She was a most artless, natural poetess. From others' poems she caught little inspiration, although Gœthe's and Schiller's works came as a blessing to her home. Sitting at her spinning-wheel she learned many of Schiller's ballads. But she caught her inspiration rather from the beautiful Alpine world around her. As Koch in his History of German Hymns says, "She had few means of instruction except the Book of Books and the book of nature. Both of these she had studied diligently, and the deep insight she obtained from both is shown in her poems." Even before she had read Klopstock, who was the inspirer of so many German poets, she felt the impulse to write, which she could not suppress. She wrote her poems as the outbursts of her heart, little dreaming of their publication. But her friends, especially Knapp, of Stuttgard, thought otherwise, and wanted them put in print. For a long time she refused to make public these "spirit children" as she called them. Finally, Knapp, in 1834, secured permission to print a few over the signature of "A Hidden One," in his Christoterpe. These gave her fame. In 1857 he succeeded in getting her to allow him to publish the first volume of her poems, followed ten years later by a second volume. In a short time she was known wherever the German language was spoken. Her husband died in 1859, and she spent the remaining years of her life at her beautiful eagle's eyrie at Hirzel with two of her daughters. She died January 2, 1876. "O come, Lord, Jesus," she said. And as her sister, Anna, asked her, "You are glad to enter heaven, are you not?" she replied, "O, yes," and she passed beyond the clouds and above the Alps to Christ's throne of glory. One of the most pleasant visits the writer has made in Europe was to Hirzel to see Meta Heusser's grave, and meet her daughter. "This is the room," the daughter said to me, "where Dr. Schaff loved to spend his time and where my mother died,"—a room overlooking the beautiful lake of Zurich. Dr. Schaff was a warm friend of the poetess, and when in Europe always visited there.

Some of her poems were translated into English and published in a little booklet called Alpine Lyrics. Fortunately her poetry is so simple as to be easily rendered into English. We give one of her poems to show their peculiar beauty. It reveals how nature, and especially the Alps, inspired her poetry:

The everlasting hills; how calm they rise,
Bold witnesses to an almighty God.
We gaze with longing heart and eager eyes,
And feel as if short pathway may suffice
From those pure regions to the heavenly land.

At early dawn when the first rays of light,
Play like a rose wreath in the peaks of snow,
And late, when half the valley seems in night,
Yet still, around each pale majestic height,
The sun's last smile has left a crimson glow.

Then the heart longs, it calls for wings to fly
Above all lower scenes of earth to soar,
Where yonder golden clouds arrested lie,
Where granite cliffs and glaciers gleam on high,
As with reflected light from heaven's door.

Whence the strange spell, by thoughtful souls confessed,
Even in shadow of the mountains found?
'Tis the deep voice within our human breast,
Which bids us seek a refuge and a rest
Above, beyond, what meets us here around.

Ever to men of God the hills were dear,
Since on the slopes of Ararat, the dove
Plucked the wet olive, pledge of hope and cheer,
Or Israel stood entranced in silent fear,
While God on Sinai thundered from above.

And once on Tabor was a vision given,
Sublime as that which Israel feared to view.
When the transfigured Lord of earth and heaven,
Mortality's dim curtain lifted, riven,
Revealed His glory to His chosen few.

On mountain heights of Galilee he prayed
While others slept, and all beneath was still;
From Olivet's recesses of awful shade
Thrice was that agonized petition made,
"O that this cup might pass, if such thy will!"

And on Mount Zion, in the better land,
Past every danger of the pilgrim way,
At our Redeemer's feet we hope to stand
And learn the meanings of His guiding hand
Through all the changes of our earthly day.

Then hail, calm sentinels of heaven, again
Proclaim your message, as in ages past!
Tell us that pilgrims shall not toil in vain,
That Zion's mount we surely shall attain,
Where all home longings find a home at last.

A. Knapp, one of the finest literary critics of German poetry, says of her: "An admirable writer, whose tender spiritual lays far surpass those of former German poetesses. She knows alike how to breathe the flute tones of faith or to sound the trumpet call among the children of God." Rev. Dr. Schaff says: "Her poems combine true poetic genius with deep piety and experience in the school of affliction, which impart to them an air of holy sadness and home-longings after heaven and thus render them peculiarly consoling to sad hearts."

Chapter II.—WOMEN OF AMERICA.

I.

MRS. THOMAS C. DOREMUS.

ONE American lady may be added, in closing this record of the Reformed women. She did not live in the days of martyrdom and suffering, but in the times of the larger development of the Christian activities. It was the mission of the women of past centuries to sustain the church; of the women of today, to extend the church in its influence. In this widening sphere of the new opportunity for woman offered in the last century Mrs. Thomas C. Doremus, of New York City, has left a most remarkable and noble record.

She was born in New York City, but her parents removed in her childhood to Elizabeth, N. J. In 1821 she was married to Mr. Thomas C. Doremus, who cordially sympathized with all her Christian activities, and by his princely liberality as long as he was able, aided her in sustaining them. She united with the Dutch Reformed church of New York about 1822, and though a devoted adherent of the Reformed faith, yet her sympathy knew no sect; her catholic spirit knew no dividing lines.

Her interest in foreign missions she dated back to her girlhood in 1812, when her mother would take her to meetings where Mrs. Isabella Graham and others would pray for the conversion of the world. The ladies of the various congregations were then accustomed to prepare outfits for missionaries and often she went to Boston where they usually embarked, and fitted up their rude cabins with the comforts for the voyage and added tempting delicacies. And when the missionaries returned, often broken down in health she would place her most delicate dainties on the table, saying, "It is because they do not get this that I want them to enjoy it now." On one occasion a returned missionary happened to lament to her that in the outfit for a voyage to India only cotton sheets had been provided for a delicate husband. Mrs. Doremus immediately applied to several friends for linen sheets. When she was asked to take them to the missionary, she replied, "Send them yourself in your own name, as she will appreciate deeply this expression of your personal interest." The next day the missionary said to Mrs. Doremus, "My dear friend, do you know the most wonderful thing happened after I mentioned to you my disappointment about the cotton sheets. Ring after ring came to our door and every one was to bring linen sheets." Years afterwards, when an occasion called for a repetition of this incident, Mrs. Doremus said, "I never told my friend that I had asked for them."

Far away in a southern parsonage a minister's wife happened to meet a returned missionary from Persia, brought together through the forethought of Mrs. Doremus. When this missionary arrived in England, she was welcomed by Mrs. Ranyard, the head of the Bible Woman's Mission, who in their brief interview would often say, "You will know this or that when you see Mrs. Doremus," "How shall I know her," "Who is she," this lady would say to herself. She then crossed the ocean and arrived at New York and was waiting with one missionary friend while another looked up quarters for them. She knew no one, expected no one, was a lonely, bereaved stranger—all her surroundings comfortless and dreary—when a lady entered, looked here and there as if seeking some one, and at length asked if she could be directed where to find a lady whom she named, who was a returned missionary. She then went up to this strange missionary, introduced herself as Mrs. Doremus, and invited her and her companion to her house. This being declined she asked them to name an hour when she could call for them. At the appointed hour she came with a carriage to take them on a drive, but bringing a copy of the memoir, just published, of the missionary's husband, a touching surprise to this young widow on her return to America. Thus it was that she refreshed the missionaries.

She took a deep interest in the establishment of a mission in the Hawaiian Islands. Hearing that there was danger of closing the schools, she tried to raise funds to keep them open. Her husband bought for her at that time an elegant shawl of the latest fashion. She, however, begged him to give her its cost instead. With this money she purchased materials for the delicate fancy work and embroidery, in which she excelled, and prepared a box for sale in the Sandwich Islands which brought five hundred dollars.

In 1828, when the sympathies of this country went out so strongly for Greece, Mrs. Doremus, hearing of the needs of the Greek ladies, organized the ladies into a band of relief. As a result Dr. Jonas King was sent to Athens with large supplies. This opened the way for him to become missionary for many years at that port. In 1832, when Rev. Dr. Abeel of the Dutch Reformed Church, returned to the country, he tried to organize a woman's missionary society. He had made a similar appeal to the women of Great Britain, describing to them the fearful degradation of the women in the Orient. Mrs. Doremus entered into this work with great earnestness. A meeting for the purpose of organizing a Woman's Missionary Society was called at the house of Mrs. Divie Bethune. Rev. Dr. Anderson, one of the secretaries of the American Board, was present but asked the ladies to defer the organization as he feared it would interfere with the work of their Board. Mrs. Bethune answered him, "What, are the American Board afraid that the ladies will get ahead of them?" Owing to Dr. Anderson's objection, there at once appeared a division among them. Some were in favor of going on, others out of respect for Dr. Anderson wanted to wait. Then it was that Dr. Abeel made his impassioned plea, as tears rolled down his face: "What is to become of the souls of those who are ignorant of the offers of mercy and of the Bible?" So the organization of the society was postponed. But in 1860 the Woman's Foreign Missionary Society was organized. For fifteen years Mrs. Doremus' house was its headquarters and contained all the machinery necessary to do the work. And she was a mother to all the missionaries sent out by their society, helping them at their departure and welcoming them on their return. She was constantly thoughtful of their comfort though far away. She would gather items of interest, or sketches of lectures and send them to them in the field to lighten their loneliness or toil. No great public event transpired that she did not send copies of the newspapers to all the stations. And she was always looking out for inspiring books which she would send to them by mail.

But she was not only intensely interested in foreign missions, but in home missions as well, especially in city mission work. About 1835 she began a Sabbath service in the city prison of New York, and by personal work rescued many a wandering soul. Her family often heard her say, that many whom she has since seen in their carriages, she had restored to their families. Out of this prison work of hers grew her interest in the Women's Prison Association, of which she was president for fourteen years. She was for thirty-six years a manager of the City and Tract Mission Society, and for twenty-eight years a manager of the City Bible Society. She was one of the founders of the House and School of Industry and for ten years its president; and for twenty-three years connected with the Nursery and Child's Hospital.

In 1855 she took special interest in the Woman's Hospital, the first institution of the kind in the world. After Dr. Sims, who originated the idea, had been repeatedly disappointed, he came to Mrs. Doremus with his project. Although she had her hands full of other work she could not resist this plea. To none of her benevolent institutions did she devote as much work as to this, often going to Albany to secure charter or State appropriations, and collecting large sums for it. She early began Sabbath religious services in the institution, and was often disappointed at the last moment in getting a minister. She would then start out early Sunday morning in search of one, sometimes getting to church breathless, saying, "I have secured a minister." After the hospital service she would distribute tracts and leaflets to the patients with words of cheer. During the Civil War she was very busy in distributing supplies to all the hospitals in and around New York City. One very warm day a large detachment of wounded officers came unexpectedly while she was at work in the city hospital in the park. She saw their distress for handkerchiefs and immediately purchased and hemmed with her own hands dozens for their supply. She was deeply interested in the Presbyterian Home for Aged Women, and also in the infant school of her own church. With all these varied activities she did not forget her own home which always had the first claim upon her time and strength. One wonders how she ever was able to be busy in so many directions. She must have been a woman of remarkable tact and energy.

She was active to the very last. On January 22d, 1877, she had a fall against the furniture of her house which was a premonition of her death. Yet the Saturday before her injury she distributed the annual prizes at the Home and School of Industry to the poor children. On the last Sabbath she spent on earth, she sent through her daughter the gifts to the patients of the Woman's Hospital, and on her return listened with eagerness to her account of their reception by the inmates. She died January 29, 1877, greatly mourned by all and greatly missed by the societies she had aided.

There were two secrets to her wonderful life, personal consecration and untiring activity. Thus when the Woman's Missionary Society met at her house and she was asked if this or that could be done, her reply was, "All I have is the Lord's." For her to live was Christ. A friend once met her at the Moody meetings in the Hippodrome and greeted her with, "Are you here alone?" Her reply was, "No, I am never alone." That was the secret of her life—the continual presence of her Lord with her. Her activity was as great as her consecration. Her favorite text was, "Whatsoever thy hand findeth to do, do it with thy might." As her health was generally delicate and she suffered for many years from pulmonary troubles, she often said, "I do today, for fear tomorrow will never come." Rev. Dr. E. P. Rogers, her pastor at the South Dutch church, said in his funeral address as he bent over her form lying before the pulpit, "For the first time she rests from her labors. He beautifully said in that address: "Well, here is her epitaph, written 1800 years ago by St. Paul, 'Well reported of for good works, she hath hath brought up children, she hath lodged strangers, she hath washed the saints' feet, she hath relieved the afflicted, she hath diligently followed every good work.'"

Other Related Titles from Solid Ground Christian Books

In addition to *Famous Women of the Reformed Church* we are honored to offer several titles for the woman of God.

Stepping Heavenward by Elizabeth Prentiss has been a favorite of women all over the world since it first appeared 140 years ago. It is fictional journal of one woman's journey from this world to the next. Elisabeth Elliot wrote the Foreword.

More Love to Thee: The Life & Letters of Elizabeth Prentiss by George Lewis Prentiss is the moving biography of gifted servant of God.
"It reveals the character of a woman who loved God and earnestly sought to help others to love Him." - Elisabeth Elliot

Golden Hours: Heart-Hymns of the Christian Life by Elizabeth Prentiss is the rarest of her works. "Elizabeth Prentiss did not squander her suffering... In this gem of a book, she gives us a glimpse not only of the treasures she mined but of her darkness, providing a backdrop against which those treasures sparkle all the more brightly. What a gift!" – Susan Hunt

Mothers of the Wise and Good by Jabez Burns was the very first title published by Solid Ground back in early 2001. This new edition is the best ever published. In the words of John Angell James, "It is a useful and valuable work, replete with instruction and encouragement...it deserves to have a wide circulation."

The Mother at Home: Raising Your Children in the Fear of the Lord by John Abbott is a classic that should be read by every mother.

Woman Her Mission and Her Life by Adolphe Monod, who is best known for his book *Monod's Farewell* which was published most recently by Banner of Truth. Monod was considered the most gifted preacher in the Reformed Church in France. This volume is the substance of two sermons preached to the congregation in Paris in February 1848.

The Excellent Woman as Described in Proverbs by Anne Pratt is one of our latest titles for women. It is introduced by William B. Sprague, who said, "the more widely it is circulated, the better for the country and the world."

My Mother – A Story of Maternal Influence by John Mitchell is a precious account of the lasting influence a godly mother can have upon her family, and the world. "It is one of those rare pictures painted from life with the exquisite skill of one of the old masters, which so seldom present themselves to the amateur."

Old Paths for Little Feet by Carol Brandt is a manual to assist both mothers and grandmothers in the glorious task of training little ones for God.

Call us Toll Free at **1-866-789-7423**
Visit our web site at **www.solid-ground-books.com**

Printed in the United States
126107LV00008B/35/A